MW00647297

The Tale of Two Horses

A 10,000 mile journey as told by the horses

Aimé Tschiffely

The Long Riders' Guild Press

www.thelongridersguild.com

ISBN: 978-1-59048-297-1

To the Reader:

The editors and publishers of The Long Riders' Guild Press faced significant technical and financial difficulties in bringing this and the other titles in the Equestrian Travel Classics collection to the light of day.

Though the authors represented in this international series envisioned their stories being shared for generations to come, all too often that was not the case. Sadly, many of the books now being published by The Long Riders' Guild Press were discovered gracing the bookshelves of rare book dealers, adorned with princely prices that placed them out of financial reach of the common reader. The remainder were found lying neglected on the scrap heap of history, their once-proud stories forgotten, their once-glorious covers stained by the toil of time and a host of indifferent previous owners.

However The Long Riders' Guild Press passionately believes that this book, and its literary sisters, remain of global interest and importance. We stand committed, therefore, to bringing our readers the best copy of these classics at the most affordable price. The copy which you now hold may have small blemishes originating from the master text.

We apologize in advance for any defects of this nature.

THE
TALE OF TWO HORSES

"Gato"

"Mancha"

CONTENTS

CONTENTS

THE
TALE OF TWO HORSES

"ANIMALI PARLANTI"

EVEN had the book been by "Ingenious Porta writ," it could not have made the conversations of the two protagonists more natural. The author has endowed them with human speech; but he has not, as many writers have done, given them a human point of view.

They remain, Mancha and Gato, two Patagonian horses, simple and lovable.

Of course, the writer has an advantage over most other writers, who have made animals fabulate. The two-and-a-half years of intimate companionships have made him, as it were, one with them. He has as completely entered into their souls as they, I feel sure, have entered into his. No one can think of him without at the same time thinking of Mancha and Gato. No one can think of them without at the same time thinking of the writer. They are as much part and parcel of one another, as are the three Persons of the Trinity.

Once more the trio traverse the Pampa, scale the Bolivian Andes, struggle through Peruvian sands, cross swinging bridges, swim crocodile-infested rivers, and brave the dangers of the super road-hogs of the United States.

They shiver amongst Andian snows, swelter in Atacama and the Canal Zone, endure short commons, want of water, and the assaults of every kind of insect and of vampire bats.

The journey is the same, but, as told by those equine masters of the pen, Mancha and Gato, it becomes quite different.

Somehow or other, they or their interpreter have endowed it with a peculiar charm. The self-same episodes, told from a different angle, take on a different air.

Naturally the horses' minds are chiefly occupied with food, as are the minds of thousands of our fellow-Christians.

The difference between them is, that horses eat to live, the taxables I have referred to, live, as it seems, to eat.

How he has managed it I do not know, but "The Master," as his two friends call him, has avoided all taint of that sentimentality by which so many of our countrymen descend into the pit. Perhaps it is his nationality that saves him, for no one in his wildest dreams can conjure up a sentimental Swiss. One thing emerges clearly from this re-telling of the tale. The rider suffered far more than the horses.

Malaria, dysentery, and El Soroche (mountain sickness) made his trip at times a burden. His horses never were sick or sorry for a single day. The wiry, salitrose grasses of the northern Pampa, straw, rotten hay, fresh maize-stalks, and the leaves of the palm-tree called Pindó, they ate and seemed to thrive upon. Changes of water did not seem to disagree with them. No horse of any other breed would have endured the hardships that they took in their stride.

The book is said to be for children, but children of ripe years may find much in its pages to mark, learn and inwardly digest.

"Pawky" asides, I write the Scoticism with trembling, under the eyes of stylists, abound; adventures crop up, so inevitably that they scarce seem adventures, till one re-reads them. The curious account of how in Mexico they lasso crocodiles, diving down to where they have their lairs, a feat I have often heard

of, but never seen performed, scarcely astonishes, it is told so
simply, through the horses' mouths.

It all seems easy, but then, "quel facile, cuanto é difficile!"
Another time, they all join in a hunt after some bandits,
surprise them, and take two prisoners, "they were hung
immediately!"

Of course they were. It neither shocks nor yet astonishes us.
True, it occurred in the same State of Mexico, to whose governor
the President sent the admonition not to hang bandits along the
side of the high roads. "It is," he said, "a most insanitary
practice, and scares off tourists."

Skilfully the writer makes his literary partners responsible for
his own ideas. Quite innocently, they have a sly hit now and
then against several of the well-known fetishes, that are
worshipped by the world. The noise, the hurry and the nothing-
ness of life in cities excites the wonder of the Patagonian
philosophers, but so subtly that it is difficult to make out to
which of the three literary units to attribute the reflexions.
Personally I give my vote to Mancha, for we know on good
authority that Gato was chiefly occupied with forage, and
"Master" knows all too well what is due to a collaborator, to
obtrude his own opinions in a joint piece of literature.

One thing is certain, that the illustrations, striking and
original, are the work of "Master," for even free-hand drawing
is not taught in the Tolderia of the Cacique Lempichun, the
former owner of the horses.

His studies in the art practised by Matisse and Apelles never
got further than painting horses' brands. Following the example
of the older masters of the art, the Chief used to prepare him-

self, the surface on which he had to paint. After some cogitation, he would smooth the sand out carefully. Then with a brown and dirty finger, or the point of his long knife, inscribe his masterpieces on the ground. On rare occasions he would burn them with a hot iron, upon the door, which he used as his Record Office. When future generations of the intelligent in such matters are in a difficulty, as to the brands of the two equine authors of this book, they will find the labours of the Chief invaluable.

Master and his two co-adjutors seem to have found the trail through the United States both dangerous and uninteresting.

The return journey to the "querencia"; the crowds at Buenos Aires to welcome home the wanderers, and the opening of the "potrero" gates, when Master let his two companions loose once more to roam their native sea of grass, is "emocionante" in its simplicity. I felt the joy of the two horses right to the marrow of the bones. And as for Master, I accompany him in his grief, when he turned in the saddle to see the last of his old friends.

As to a heaven with harps, and angels casting down their golden crowns to slither on the glassy sea, like curling stones upon the ice, I take it, as we say in Scottish law, ad avisandum. But there must be a Trapalanda, an equine paradise where only horses and the men who loved them are admitted; where spur-marks, saddle-sores, splints, spavins, ring-bone, broken wind, and all the ills that hard work and ill-treatment have inflicted on man's partner in the taming of the world, are blotted out and quite forgotten, I feel certain. If not, Eden itself would have been but the cruel jest of a malign and evil deity.

R. B. CUNNINGHAME GRAHAM.

In which Mancha talks about his wild homeland

I WAS born far, far away, in a place called Patagonia, which, as you probably know, is way down at the southern end of South America. When I was a baby—or a *colt*, as you call a very young horse —I scampered about with a big herd of wild horses. Although the place where I was born is almost a desert, and icy winds from the cold regions near the South Pole sweep over the sandy plains and barren rocky hills, I love my homeland. Some people think that it's hot everywhere in South America, but they are wrong. My birthplace is far away to the south of the equator. Down there we have long winters when deep snow covers the mountains, hills and plains.

Oh, how I hated those winters! Many a day and night the wild south wind whirled snow around us, making me seek shelter behind my mother. How miserable and hungry we were sometimes! When we wanted to eat we had to scratch away the snow till we found the withered grass below; and even if we were lucky enough to find some, there was but very little of it.

You see, we wild horses have what you call *instinct*, which makes it possible for us to know where there is grass; even if we can't see it.

Sometimes we were so starved that we had to eat dry twigs and shrubs. I have even seen horses in our herd who were so hungry that they nibbled off each other's manes and tails.

Still, in spite of these hard winters, we kept alive; and I slowly grew up to be a strong and big horse.

If you had seen me when I was a colt you would probably have thought that I looked very funny, for my coat was all dark red and white blotches, and I had a short, scraggy tail and long legs, like four animated stilts.

Perhaps you don't know why colts have such long legs, so I will tell you the reason.

I've already said that I used to be a wild horse, so if you bear this in mind you can easily imagine how difficult it must have been for me to keep up with the herd when all the horses galloped fast and far. If my legs had been short I could never have done it, and would have been left behind to die of starvation or thirst, or to be eaten by enemies who often prowled about. We were always looking out for Indians and *pumas,* as the South American lions are called.

I vividly remember seeing one of these fierce and cunning beasts of prey leap on the back of one of my playmates who had gone too far away from the herd. Poor little fellow! How he screamed! We were so frightened that we galloped away as fast as we could, and as I kept pressing against my mother, I was glad that I had such long legs. When I thought I could gallop no longer, the herd stopped, and while all the horses snorted excitedly, my mother sniffed and licked me affectionately. Although the mother of my poor playmate called him for several days, he never returned. This taught me never to stray too far away from the herd.

By degrees I learned to know by smelling when there were

enemies about; and I'm sure that this instinct must have saved my life more than once.

I was nearly a year old when I saw a man for the first time, but I will tell you about this later. I've done a lot of talking already, so now I'll let my pal *Gato* say a few words.

STORY TWO

What Gato has to say about his family

MY name is *Gato*, which is the Spanish word for *cat*. When I was young I had no name, but after I was captured by men and tamed, my master called me Gato because the colour of my coat is the same as that of many cats; dark-brown with black stripes.

Since Mancha didn't tell you why he was given his name, I'll do it for him. He talks such a lot that he often forgets what he started out to say. If he had been a schoolboy he would have given his masters a lot of trouble, and wouldn't have been much good at his lessons. He is a scatter-brain and is much too lively to stand still and think. *Mancha* means *stain* or *spot*. You already know that my pal's coat is just one mass of big and small golden-red and white blotches; so now, I'm sure, you can easily guess why he is called *Mancha*.

I also was born in Patagonia, and belonged to the same herd as Mancha did, but I'm two years younger than he is. Now I'm getting on in years, and, having seen a great deal of the world, I really know quite a lot for a horse.

Mancha has already told you something about our home and friends, and now I'll say a little about my family, which is very, very old.

Some of you human beings may be very proud of your old families, but none of you can ride the high horse when we begin to talk about *our* ancestors.

The family-tree of us horses goes back at least fifty million years. Our earliest ancestors are called "dawn horses." When they lived the world looked quite different. In many places there were huge swamps, and the air was steamy and much warmer than it is now. Everywhere grew big leafy plants which were eaten by strange and terrifying monsters which, in their turn, were devoured by others who were bigger and fiercer than they.

The *dawn horses* were only about the size of big cats. They had arched backs, and feet which were rather big for their size. On the fore-feet they had four toes, and three on each hind-foot. These big feet prevented them from sinking into the soft ground.

Slowly, as thousands and thousands of years passed, the swamps gradually dried, grass-lands and forests taking their place; and by degrees, as the world changed, so did our ancestors —the *dawn horses*. They grew bigger and bigger until they were the size of Newfoundland dogs. The ground had become much harder, and therefore they no longer needed so many toes to prevent them from sinking into the mud and slime. In consequence our remote ancestors' feet slowly changed until they had only three toes on each foot, and the two side ones were getting smaller also.

Again thousands of years passed, and our ancestors grew bigger and bigger. They learned to walk on tiptoe, and slowly hoofs began to grow to protect the delicate bones which had to carry all their weight. By degrees the side toes nearly disappeared, for they were no longer needed. When our forefathers had grown to the size of a pony and had developed hoofs, they began to look much more like we do to-day. All the horses you know still have something of the side toes of our ancestors left, but they are now buried in the flesh, and you call them *splint-bones*.

Our forefathers still kept on growing, and as they could no longer hide in the forests—which had disappeared in many places—they now lived in the prairies where they learned to eat grass instead of soft leaves. They had many enemies who hunted them, so they were obliged to run very fast to save themselves.

Again thousands of years passed, and finally our forefathers changed so much in appearance that they looked almost like we do now.

Some men who know a lot about prehistoric animals say that my early ancestors lived on the American continent; and people have even found bones of early horses, which they have placed in museums.

For some unknown reason all the horses died out in America; and when Columbus discovered the continent, not a single one lived there, and even the Red Indians didn't remember that such an animal had once upon a time existed in their land. When the natives first saw white men riding on horses they fled in terror, thinking they were strange monsters with two heads.

Shortly after the discovery of America, the Spaniards brought over several ships full of horses. Some of these were turned loose on the prairies of North America, while others were shipped to far-away South America where they were freed and allowed to roam over the *pampas*. *Pampa* is an old Indian word meaning *space*—a most appropriate name for the vast plains which look just like an endless green ocean.

The horses which were turned loose by the Spaniards soon raised big families, and these, in their turn, increased so much that—after a number of years—herds consisting of thousands roamed about, and when they galloped their hoofs made a noise which sounded like the rumbling of thunder.

Although the Indians were terrified when they saw the first horses with riders on them, they soon found out that they were not monsters with two heads, and that horses were much less to be feared than the white men who had come to invade their country. It didn't take the natives long to realise how useful horses are, and before long they captured some and learnt to ride so well that they became better horsemen than the Spaniards.

To catch my ancestors, the Pampas Indians used three balls they fixed to the ends of leather thongs which were tied together in the shape of a star, with a ball at each point. This dangerous weapon is called *boleadoras* or *bolas*. When it is thrown at a

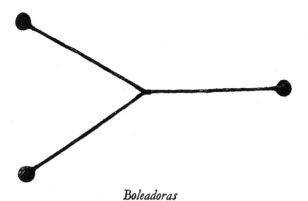

Boleadoras

horse's legs, the three balls wrap themselves round them, making escape impossible. The Indians use the *bolas* for fighting men, and also to hunt wild animals.

After a very short time the horses—which had been turned loose by the Spaniards—became quite wild, and were called *mesteños,* but later, the cowboys, who could not speak Spanish, twisted the word into *mustang.*

Mancha has already told you that he and I were wild horses when we were young, so now, you see, that we are really South American mustangs.

STORY THREE

How Mancha saw men for the first time, and lost his mother

I DIDN'T worry about anything till I was about a year old, but just about then I had the biggest fright in all my life.

Spring had arrived, and the snow had already melted on the plains of Patagonia, but the mountains and hills were still covered with a mantle of white, which, in the bright sunshine, glittered like a mass of diamonds. Down on the plain the sun was so warm that I lay down to enjoy it for a while after I had had a good game with some other colts. Half asleep, I could hear the grown-up horses munching grass, and every now and again my mother came to sniff me or to lick my coat where it was rough. I was just beginning to sleep when I heard excited snorts. I quickly rose and pushed against my mother, who held her head high and looked towards the distant horizon. There was nothing to be seen but the plain, and white clouds which slowly drifted towards us; but I guessed that something must be amiss, for the snorts the horses gave were snorts of warning. I wondered if a puma were prowling about, or if it were some other enemy, for the herd was getting very nervous—a sure sign that something was amiss.

When I looked in the direction in which my mother gazed, I saw some tiny specks in the distance. The wind was blowing towards us from the south, and after a while I smelt a strange smell. Something seemed to tell me that this must come from an

9

enemy; or else, why should the whole herd be so excited?

Nearer and nearer drew those specks, which, as they approached, looked like horses to me. I couldn't understand why my mother and all our friends should be so scared, and it seemed strange to me that the horses in the distance had such a peculiar smell.

All of a sudden my herd started to gallop away in terror. On and on we raced, as fast as we could. After a while, in front of us, appeared other horses with strange humps on their backs.

In a flash we all turned round and started to run back, but we had not gone far when the horses we had first run away from came racing towards us. To my surprise I then noticed that they also had some queer things on their backs, and I thought these strange humps moved as if they were alive. I squealed with fear as we turned to flee in another direction, and my heart thumped till I thought it would burst.

Closer and closer came the strange horses, and soon we were almost surrounded by them. The trampling of hoofs and the snorting terrified me, and, to make things worse, there was so much dust that I could no longer see where I was going. I don't remember how long the stampede lasted, but suddenly I crashed into a heap of falling and struggling horses, and then there was such a mix-up that I don't know what happened. I heard snorts and squeals of terror, and I was frantically struggling to save myself from being trampled on or kicked.

When, at last, I was able to rise, I was caught in an avalanche of other horses who were madly racing round in a small circle. I was being bumped and pushed around till I thought all the bones in my body must be broken; and when I tried to run out of this whirlpool of horses, I crashed into a row of high posts, which I hadn't been able to see owing to the thick cloud of dust. Half stunned, I joined the horses who were still milling round and rearing up. After a while I noticed that we were running in a small circle because we were surrounded by posts, and presently I saw what I thought must be strange animals which were on the other side of these posts.

Getting tired, we gradually stopped running in a circle, and then I had a good look at the strange animals who were watching us with piercing eyes. To my amazement they stood on their hind-legs, and every now and again they made peculiar noises with their mouths. I was used to the neighing and nickering of horses, I had heard the roaring of wild beasts, and was familiar with the noises birds and many other animals make; but the sounds these strange beings made were quite different. When they looked at me with their mysterious eyes, I felt quite helpless and was so frightened that I shook and quivered like a bird's feathers in a gale.

Now I'll tell you what were these strange and terrifying beings who walked on two legs—Indians! Men!

After a while—it seemed like a long winter—the Indians came nearer and threw long ropes with loops at the ends at some of us. When these loops fell over the head or around the neck of a horse he was caught in it, and although he struggled for dear life, he couldn't get away, for he was *lassoed*.

Having caught about twenty horses, the Indians opened the corral in which we were trapped, and let us out. How we galloped! On and on we raced till it was dark, and when we finally stopped I looked for my mother, whom I had not seen from the time I had crashed into that heap of horses. All night long I searched for her among the herd. I called and called, but there came no reply. Several other colts were also looking for their mothers. Some were lucky and found them, but I, like a few other unfortunate ones, never saw my dear mother again; for she was so beautiful that the Indians must have caught her, probably to spend the rest of her life in slavery.

On our wild flight several very young colts who could not keep up with the herd were left behind, and although their mothers called them for several days, only two or three came back. The others were lost for ever.

STORY FOUR

Gato tells the tale of his childhood

MANCHA was already two years old when I was born. I had many colts to play with, so, in those days, I only knew Mancha by sight and smell. You already know that we horses know men, animals, plants, and many other things by their odour, and that —thanks to our sensitive noses—we can often smell danger long before we see it. Most of you human beings have forgotten how to make use of your noses, but perhaps this is just as well, for I still snort in disgust when I remember being taken into cities and villages. Phew! What smells! And the men didn't even seem to notice them!

However, I shall come to this later, so, for the moment, I will tell you a little about my childhood.

My father, who was a very powerful and good-looking mustang, had lots of wives—I think there must have been about fifty of them. If ever a strange stallion came along and tried to flirt with any of my father's wives, there was a terrible fight which never ended till the intruder was driven away. When Father finished with these strangers they took good care never to return, for it must have taken weeks before all the bruises and cuts had healed where they had been bitten and kicked.

My father was always on the look-out for danger. Whilst his wives and children grazed or rested, he usually stood somewhere near where the ground was highest, and there, with his

13

proud head held high, he looked as far as he could and sniffed the air. Whenever an enemy appeared, he was first to see him, and when he gave his shrill neigh of warning, the whole herd galloped away with the speed of the wind.

On our plains there are many animals and birds which are friendly with us horses. One kind of little bird is a special friend of ours, for when ticks and other vermin crawl on us to suck our blood, these birds hop on our backs and eat them.

We are so used to our feathered friends—which look something like brown wag-tails—that we don't mind it a bit when they hop all over our backs, all the time picking ticks and other insects off us.

Among the many other birds and animals I used to know were ostriches, armadillos, hares and *guanacos* which look rather like very big deer with long and upright necks.

I could go on telling you for hours about the strange animals I know, but it would take much too long. Still, I must tell you something about ostriches, for their way of raising a family is very strange.

All the female ostriches lay their eggs in one big nest, which is just a hollow in the ground. Sometimes there are as many as thirty huge eggs in the same nest. When the female ostrich has finished laying her eggs she just walks away, and one of the males makes it his duty to sit on the nest till the eggs are hatched. In due time the fluffy and long-legged baby ostriches come out of the eggs, and then the same male who has been sitting on the nest does the duty of father, mother and nurse. All the little ostriches follow him, and he teaches them what grasses and grubs to eat. The female ostriches never even trouble to look at their children; in fact, they don't even bother to find out if the eggs they have laid were fertile or not.

Some of the big lizards I got to know later in life are even stranger than the ostriches. They lay their eggs in dry sand, and the sun does the hatching. When the young lizards finally come out of the eggs they at once scratch their way to the surface of the sand. Before they come out it is just as well for them to peep out carefully, for if their own parents happen to see them they will gobble them up in a jiffy. There are surely some strange families in this world!

I set out to tell you about my childhood, and I suddenly find myself gossiping about other families. Now, let's go back to where I left off.

After my mother had given birth to another colt she took but little notice of me, for I was old enough to look after myself, and, besides, she was much too busy with my little sister to be bothered with me as well. You see, when we horses are a year old our mothers tell us that we are big and strong enough to find our own living.

Three years passed, and being a big horse now, I joined Mancha's gang, which I thought was the nicest and liveliest in the herd. Mancha was a terrible fellow in those days—always fighting and looking for trouble. For the first few days he bullied me quite a lot, but soon we became good friends and were always to be seen together.

Mancha tells a story about an armadillo and a fox

GATO has been talking about ostriches, lizards and other animals, so before I tell you the story about the day that changed my whole life, I must tell you an amusing legend about an armadillo and a fox.

On a lovely moonlight night an armadillo was strolling over the pampas when he met a fox who was a friend of his.

Both these animals sleep all day in their holes underground, and usually they only come out after the sun has set. That's the time when many animals go out hunting or searching for things to eat. They say *"good night"* when you say *"good morning,"* and before they go to sleep they say *"good day"!*

"Good night, Mr. Reynard," the armadillo said to the fox. "Any good hunting?"

"Good night, Mr. Armadillo," answered the fox. "A lovely night. No luck yet with my hunting, but I hope for the best. I trust Mrs. Armadillo and the kids are well?"

"Very well, Mr. Reynard. Thanks for enquiring. I hope all's well in your hole."

The two chatted for a while, and then they started to argue as to which one of them could throw the lasso better. Unable to agree, they finally decided to fetch a rope and put themselves to a test.

Not very far away, a number of horses were peacefully

grazing, and so the two rivals drew lots to decide which one was to have the first throw. The armadillo won. When he had carefully tied one end of the lasso around his armoured body, he coiled up the rest of the rope in his right fore-paw, and then slowly crept towards the unsuspecting horses. When he was near enough, and had picked his victim, he threw the lasso, the loop falling beautifully around the horse's neck.

Before you could say "Hoof!" the armadillo ran into a hole and dug his four legs into its walls of earth. When an armadillo does this you simply can't pull him out.

For some time the lassoed horse struggled to free himself, rearing up, pulling and kicking with all his strength. But it was no use, for the more he pulled the tighter did the lasso close round his neck. After a while the armadillo let go the rope, and the frightened horse galloped away as fast as he could.

The fox had been watching in the distance, and when it was his turn to show what he could do, he decided to try the armadillo's trick to hold his victim. Accordingly, he tied one end of the rope round his body and carefully coiled up the rest in his right fore-paw.

When all was ready, and the fox had picked the horse he intended to lasso, he swung the rope and cleverly threw the loop around his neck.

"Good shot!" the armadillo shouted as the fox ran into the nearest hole to hold the horse.

A fox isn't as strong in the legs as an armadillo is, so when the startled horse bolted, and the lasso suddenly tightened, the fox was pulled out of the hole with a terrible jerk; and before he had time to undo the knot, the horse raced over the prairie, dragging Mr. Reynard behind him. Goodness! How he squealed and yelled with pain and fear as he was rolling and bouncing along till he was dragged out of sight!

Armadillos can't run very fast, but—by following the trail through the dew—our friend waddled along as quickly as he could. Whenever he came to a place where the fox had lost a tuft of hair, the armadillo exclaimed, "Poor Mr. Reynard, poor Mr. Reynard! What will his wife and family say when they hear about this?"

He had been following the trail for a long time when he finally caught sight of the fox. Luckily the lasso had snapped, or else the poor animal would have been dragged to death. There he was sitting, all sore and giddy, and holding his tummy where the lasso had cut into him. He panted for air, his eyes rolled with pain, and his mouth was wide open, with the tongue lolling out—just like a dog when he has been running fast and is out of breath.

As the armadillo approached he thought the fox was laughing, so he sarcastically said, "Hi! Mr. Reynard! I really don't know what *you* can be laughing at. What bruises and lumps and what a black eye! You've lost most of your fur and half your whiskers, and—what's more—you're a rotten cowboy; and you've lost the bet!"

STORY SIX

Being Gato's account of how he and Mancha were captured
by the Indians

THERE; that's just like Mancha! Fancy laughing at the poor fox!
Just think what his wife and kiddies must have said when Mr.
Reynard came home in the morning. Nothing to eat; Daddy all
bruised and torn, and his saucy whiskers missing!

Now I'm going to tell you a sad story about the day when
we were rounded up and caught by the Indians, and then sold
to white men.

Both Mancha and I were grown-up mustangs. Although we
often had very little to eat, and sometimes even starved, we had
a lovely time with our herd. We had many good friends, and
we were very happy wild horses.

One day the Indians rounded us up. It happened and felt
much the same as Mancha told you in Story Three, in which he
gave an account of what occurred when he saw men for the first
time in his life.

Our herd was driven into a corral where some of us were
lassoed and tied to posts. When I got over my first fright and
looked around, I was glad to see that Mancha was near me.
He was tied to a post, and although he struggled desperately,
he could not free himself.

Having caught and tied up all the horses they wanted, the
Indians opened the corral and let the rest of the herd out. The

trampling of hundreds of hoofs soon died away as my beloved herd disappeared for ever behind a cloud of dust at the horizon. Every time I tried to follow my lucky friends who had been set free, I nearly pulled my head off, and the pain was so great that I stopped tugging at the rope with which I was tied.

The Indians had gone away, and when we poor prisoners were left alone we called our herd in vain. All that day, and the following night we remained tied to the posts. Every now and again there was a commotion when one of us tried to free himself, but after some time we realised that our struggles were useless; so we just stood there, sad and miserable.

If we had been human beings we would have cried, but being horses, we showed our sorrow by letting our ears hang. If people know and understand us they can always tell when we are sad, for by looking into our eyes, they can read in them our sorrow and pain. When we laugh we prick up our ears, and our eyes twinkle merrily.

Some people think that horses never laugh or feel sad, but they are silly and know nothing about us. They consider us to be stupid because we can't speak as they do, and therefore they often ill-treat us. I always feel sorry for these people, for if they could only understand us as well as we know them, they could learn a great deal from us, and we could give them much joy. However, that's another story, so let me go on telling you about the day when we were made captives, and some of us became slaves to man.

Early next morning the Indians came towards us, and I thought we would be killed. I had never seen such strange beings before, and although I did my best to get away from them I could do nothing. To my great surprise they unfastened the rope by which I was tied, and when all the other horses were freed we hoped we would be let out of the corral, but we were disappointed, for all we were allowed to do was to mill around and huddle together with fear.

I noticed that some strange men—whose colour was much whiter than the Indians'—were also on the other side of the posts, watching us. I can't tell you how frightened we were as we watched the men move about. The white men were talking with the Indians, and every now and again they pointed at us with what I then thought were their fore-legs. Now I know that they were bartering before buying us; and I still think the men had no right to sell or to buy us. But then men are more cunning than we are, and therefore have the mastery over us, and, I suppose, they think they have a right to do with animals what they like.

The white men and the Indians were talking for a long time, and before they went away, one brought a mare which was put into the corral with us. Around her neck was hung a bell which frightened us at first, but we got so used to the tinkling that we even began to like it. The mare was very nice, so we soon made friends with her.

Later in life, I found out that men often use a mare when they want to take a troop of horses over the prairies, for once the mustangs have made friends with the bell-mare—as she is called —they never leave her. At night the two fore-legs of the bell-mare are tied together with a piece of hide or rope. With this on she can only hobble along, and therefore it is impossible for her to go very far. Since all the other horses are fond of the bell-mare, and never leave her, there is no need to tie them up, for they always graze near the tinkling bell.

If we had known that this bell-mare was put into the corral to make us follow her into captivity we would have run away when we were finally let out, but we didn't know then that men are so cunning, so we stupidly followed the mare wherever the white men drove her.

STORY SEVEN

Mancha describes a long journey towards the lands where white men live

THE days we spent in that horrible corral in Patagonia were very sad ones. We were given so little to eat that we were as hungry as we had often been in the wilds when deep snow covered the ground. From where we were we could see grass on the other side of the posts, but we couldn't get to it, so all we could do was to look at it with longing.

Not far away from the corral the Indians had a few tents. You can imagine how scared we were of them till we found out that they were harmless.

In Patagonia these tents are called *toldos*, but in North America the Indians call them *wigwams*. The tribe of Indians who had captured us is named the *Tehuelche* tribe, and the chief's name was *Liempichun*, which, in English, means: *I Have Feathers*. The *toldos* the Indians lived in were very strange; and I'm sure you wouldn't care to live in one. A few posts were stuck in the ground, and over them were stretched the hides of horses and of other animals. Inside, on the ground, the Indians cooked their food. They didn't sleep in beds, but just lay on the ground and covered themselves with an old hide or a dirty blanket. The Tehuelche Indians must be as hardy as wild animals, for even in winter they go about in the snow and ice, never bothering to put on warm clothes. Even when blizzards howl through

23

Chief Liempichun and his *toldo* (tent)

their *toldos* they don't seem to care; and when big pieces of ice
are floating about in the rivers and lakes they swim for hours
in them, and when they come out of the water they don't even
dry themselves. If they have children with them, the youngsters
follow wherever the grown-up Indians go, and if a baby is so
young that it can't walk or swim, it just hangs on to its mother's
hair while she swims in water that would freeze you stiff in a
few seconds.

From the corral where we were kept prisoners, I used to watch
these Indians in their *toldos,* and at night I listened to their way

of talking. What puzzled and frightened me most was to see them sit round fires; things I had never seen before, but which I got to know very well later.

My heart thumped with joy when the corral was opened and we were let out. A number of white men—who were sitting on horses—stopped us from running towards the wilds in the south. Seeing the bell-mare turn and gallop towards the north, we all followed behind her, and the white men came chasing behind us, yelling *"hee-hoo!"* and cracking whips.

Many years ago *hee-hoo* was the war-cry of the Pampas Indians; much the same as *Whoo-pee* was the war-cry of some Indians in North America.

On and on we galloped, and when we began to tire we settled down to a slow jog-trot. Towards evening we came to a place where there was water and grass; and when the bell-mare stopped to drink, we all did the same. I was so thirsty and hungry that I almost forgot the men who had also stopped, and who were watching us from not very far away.

Like all my friends, I wanted to go back to the wilds in the south, but as the bell-mare seemed to be quite pleased to be where she was, we all stayed with her. I could hardly believe my eyes when one of the men got off his horse and walked up to our mare. All the rest of us fled till we were about a hundred yards away, and when we saw that she stood quite still as the man approached her, we watched and snorted with fear. What could this mean? The man bent down and strapped the mare's fore-legs together, tying them just above the hoofs; and, having done this, returned to his horse which wasn't in the least afraid of him. When the bell-mare tried to walk she could only hobble along, but she didn't seem to mind, and just went on grazing.

Suspicious, and unable to understand all this, we stood and watched for some time. After a while we cautiously approached to sniff her all over with curiosity, and, finding nothing wrong, settled down to eat and drink.

Having given their horses a drink, the men took off some strange things that were fixed to their mounts' backs, whereupon they turned them loose. Later on I found out that the strange bundles these horses had on their backs were saddles. Presently you'll hear how Gato and I learned about them.

When the men's horses had rolled and shaken themselves they joined us. At first we were suspicious of them, but after we had carefully sniffed them we let them graze among us. Every now and again there was a bit of a fight, for some of us would have nothing to do with these strangers who had the smell of men about them.

The white men—who were cowboys—lit a fire, and later drank something out of a little gourd into which they stuck a metal tube, through which they sucked hot water. The gourd was handed round in a circle, and every time one man had sipped out of it, another refilled it with hot water. We watched these proceedings from a distance, and as the bell-mare didn't seem to be afraid, we stayed where we were. What strange things these men were doing! Suddenly one of them went up to the fire with a big piece of meat which he began to roast, and when it was brown, all the other men squatted on the ground and started to eat it. But stranger still! When they had finished eating, they all stuck something into their mouths, and having put glowing embers to it, they sucked at what looked little sticks, and blew smoke into the air!

Three cowboys were still on their horses, and whenever one of us went too far away from the bell-mare, they drove him back. Late into the night the other men sat near the fire where they chatted and laughed until, finally, they lay down on the ground and covered themselves with blankets. Taking it in turns to sleep and watch us, three men were always on their horses throughout the night. Long before the first streaks of violet and purple announced the arrival of another day, every man had caught and saddled his horse; and when the rope with which the bell-mare's fore-legs were tied had been taken off, we were again driven towards the north.

Now I know what the *gauchos*, or South American cowboys, were drinking out of the little gourd. It was a kind of green tea they call *maté*. It's rather bitter, but the Argentine cowboys drink some of it every day, and they can do a long morning's riding without eating any breakfast if they drink some of this *maté*.

Maté and bombilla (metal tube through which the tea is sucked)

I have also found out that the men were smoking when they stuck the strange little things into their mouths and blew smoke into the air.

For nearly a whole month we were driven north over the prairies until we came to a lovely place where juicy grass grows as far as one can see.

The people I saw there were much whiter than the Indians. They didn't live in *toldos,* but in houses built of stone, wood or clay, and they wore good clothes.

Here the prairie was fenced in with posts and wire. When we were driven through the first gate we had ever seen, we were afraid, but as the bell-mare went through without fussing we followed her after a while. I could tell that she knew the place, for she sniffed the air and called to some horses who were grazing in the distance. As soon as they heard her voice, they answered and came galloping towards her.

Shortly after we had passed through the gate the cowboys closed it, and rode away towards some houses which I could see in the distance. We all thought we were free again, for we didn't realise until later that we were shut in a huge field with high wire fences all round us.

Now you know how we were made prisoners, and how we were taken far away from our herd.

STORY EIGHT

In which Gato tells how he and Mancha met the man who was to become their master

ALTHOUGH there was plenty of juicy grass in the huge field we were in, we longed to return to our herd in Patagonia. We often galloped towards the south, but when we came to the high wire fence we could go no further, so we sadly looked towards the horizon and wondered how our friends were getting on in the wilds. About thirty members of our herd were with us, and as we had become quite fond of the bell-mare, we grew less and less homesick, and gradually settled down in the new place.

On our long journey we had eaten so little that we were very thin, but with all the good grass we soon put on flesh, and our coats began to look nice and glossy.

One day the cowboys drove us into a corral, and although we dodged and fought as much as we could, we were lassoed, one by one. We were thrown to the ground, and our legs were so well tied with ropes that we couldn't even kick when a man branded a mark on each one's hind-leg with a red-hot iron.

I've seen a lot of the world, and having kept my eyes open all the time, I know that on every ranch the animals are branded. Every cattle-owner has his own mark, of which no two are alike.

It would be impossible to brand a name on a horse or a cow, and therefore every rancher has a distinctive mark, letter or sign.

Once this is branded on an animal you can see it for the rest of its life, and therefore it's very difficult to steal marked cattle without being found out.

Like Mancha and me, many cowboys can't read, but they know the different brands of all the ranches, far and near, and they know every horse, cow and bull on their own ranch, even if there are hundreds of them. Of course, they don't give every animal a name. There aren't enough to go round. Still, they have names for all the horses they ride, and the others they simply call by their colours.

As you know, no two horses are quite alike in this respect. There are blacks, whites, chestnuts, duns, greys, roans, and some are called mouse-coloured, piebald or smoked. White horses who have tiny specks all over their bodies are called *flea-bitten!* I think that's a very funny name, especially so because we horses have no fleas who hate our smell and never come near us. We have so many other colours that, if I started to tell you all the Spanish names the South American cowboys have for them, I'd never finish.

As soon as the last horse was branded, the corral was opened and we were let out into the big field. You can imagine how we ran!

For several weeks we were never disturbed, but early one morning the cowboys again drove us into the corral.

We had been waiting for a long time when several cowboys and a man we had never seen before, came towards us from the ranch-house. The stranger was wearing a big hat with a wide brim, and his skin was whiter than that of the other men. Upon looking at him more carefully, I noticed that his hair was almost of the same colour as Mancha's red blotches.

Presently this man and one of the cowboys came into the corral, and while all of us raced around, the two kept looking at us. When the man with the big hat pointed at Mancha, the cowboy swung his lasso over his head, and then the rope whizzed towards my old pal who was soon caught and tied to a post. After a while the same thing happened to me, and then all the other horses were let out. When the gate had been shut, our ropes were untied, and we were allowed to run around the corral. Soon all the men went away, leaving the two of us alone. We called our friends, who had already galloped so far away that we could only see a cloud of dust in the distance, and both of us tried desperately to get out of our prison. Mancha was in such a temper that he snorted loudly and pawed the ground, and he was so furious that the whites of his eyes showed as he tossed flecks of foam into the air.

All that day we were left in the horrible corral, and we were beginning to feel so hungry that we longingly looked at the grass on the other side of the posts.

It was nearly evening when the stranger with the big hat came walking towards us. On his back he carried a bundle of grass, and in one hand he had a big bucket which was filled with water. When the man had entered the corral he put his burdens on the ground, whereupon he spoke to us. We were terribly frightened at first, and every time he moved towards us we tried to run away. But it was no use, for all we could do was to huddle together and run into the circle of posts which surrounded us.

The man stood there for a long time. Sometimes he spoke to us, and every now and again he slowly held out a wisp of hay.

In spite of our ravenous appetites we were much too scared to take it out of his hand, but when he threw it on the ground we immediately snatched it up.

Whenever the man spoke to me he said "*Gato*," and when he said something to my pal he called him "*Mancha*." At the time, neither of us knew that these strange sounds were to be our names, but soon we got so used to them that we knew which one he called.

The stranger stayed with us till it was dark, and then he climbed over the posts and disappeared in the direction of the house. As soon as he had gone we gobbled up the hay he had left on the ground, and when we found out that the bucket wasn't dangerous, we drank the water.

Early the next morning the same man appeared with a big bundle of hay. All day long he spoke to us, and slowly followed us around the corral. Whenever he advanced we backed away from him, but after a few hours of this we felt less nervous, although, of course, we dare not let him come too near us.

This sort of thing went on for several days, until we got so used to the man that we even snatched hay out of his hand. However, we were very careful, and when he came too near we threatened to kick him, and ran away; but he was so cautious and quick that our hoofs never touched him. Of course, we didn't mean to hurt him, for we only wanted him to realise that he had no business to come too near, because we still distrusted him, and suspected that he intended to hurt us.

A week passed; and we were still shut up in the dismal corral. The only food and water we had were brought by this man, but by this time we were so used to him that we awaited his arrival every morning. When he fed us, we even let him stroke our necks, although the touch of his hand tickled terribly at first. Once he slyly tried to slip a rope around my neck, but when I discovered his intention there was trouble—and when I say *trouble,* I mean it! Still, the man was so kind that he gradually gained our confidence; and now we liked it when he called us by our names.

Knowing that he meant no harm, we became more and more friendly, and soon we didn't mind a bit when he touched us all over. Sometimes he scratched our noses or patted our necks, and later he even put blankets on our backs, but this we only allowed after he had let us sniff them all over to make sure that they were not dangerous. Of course, when first he put these blankets on us we kicked them off, but every time they fell to the ground he picked them up and slowly put them on us again. We got so tired of kicking off these blankets that we finally preferred to leave them on our backs. By degrees we became tamer and tamer, but we had a lot to learn yet, and we had many a fright till we knew more about men and the world.

For the first time a man sits on Mancha's back

ONE morning several cowboys came towards the corral, and as we nervously watched, we noticed that our master was among them.

Before I realised what all these men had come for, I was lassoed and pulled out of the corral. My legs were then tied in such a way that it was impossible for me to move or kick without falling. I was so frightened that I wasn't aware that a man strapped one of these strange things, called *saddles,* on my back. It was fixed on so tightly around my body that I could hardly breathe, and before I knew what was happening, something that was alive leapt on my back. Almost at the same instant the ropes with which my legs were bound were untied and taken off.

At first I thought the thing on my back was a puma or some other wild animal, so I arched my back and put my head between my fore-legs, and bucked for all I was worth. I fought with such terror and fury that I squealed and tried every trick I knew to throw enemies off my back.

Only wild horses know how to buck properly, for if an enemy leaps on them they must do this to shake him off, and thus save their lives. Pumas and tigers usually jump on their victims' backs and bite their necks to kill them. To throw them off, we put our heads between our fore-legs and arch our backs—like cats do when they see a dog—and then we buck as hard as we can.

I fought so furiously that I raised a cloud of dust, but every time I bucked I heard a loud "hee-hoo!" Very soon I found out that it was not a puma, but a cowboy who was sitting on my back, and I noticed that the other men were looking on and waving their hats. Realising that I simply couldn't shake off the man by bucking, I thought I'd try to flee; so I madly raced over the prairie. Every now and again I stopped suddenly, but even this didn't move the man whose whip and spurs urged me on, faster and faster.

Seeing a tree, I decided to race towards it, and there brush off the rider, but before I had gone far, two cowboys on horses came alongside me and pushed me in another direction. After a while I was so tired and out of breath that I simply could run and buck no more, so I stood still, trembling all over. I had lost the fight. The gaucho was still on my back. What a man! How he could ride!

When I had been guided back to the corral, the saddle was taken off me and placed on Gato, whose resistance was also in vain.

Although I was dripping with perspiration, and shaking all over with exhaustion, I watched what was happening to my pal outside.

He fought so bravely that all our friends in the wilds would have been very proud of him, but again the man proved to be a good rider—and poor Gato also lost his fight. Puffing and panting and with flecks of foam all over him, he was brought back into the corral, and when the cowboys had gone, and we had

D

cooled off a little, the two of us had a long talk about our latest experience with men.

For a few days after this we were saddled and ridden. We soon realised that our riders intended to do us no harm; and as it was no use struggling against them, we slowly gave in. Once or twice we managed to throw off the rider, but he always fell on his feet like a cat, and before we had time to run away he was on our backs again.

Very soon we gave up bucking, and, instead, trotted or cantered in whatever direction our riders guided us.

When we were not being ridden we were kept in the corral; and we began to wonder if we would ever be let out again to join our pals who were happily grazing outside in the big field.

Somehow we felt that something was to happen soon, and as the days passed we felt this more and more.

STORY TEN

Gato tells how he and Mancha were brought into a huge city

OUR master was with us every day, and often took us far afield over the prairies, where thousands of cattle were grazing. One morning, before the first daylight appeared, he came to the corral, and when he had fixed the saddle on me he fastened a rope to Mancha's halter. Having done this, he patted me on the neck, and then mounted and guided us over the plains towards the north. When we had passed through several gates we came to a wide road—just a narrow strip of prairie between two wire fences—which led straight north, over the flat country. Every now and then we saw a dead cow or horse, but although we were afraid and snorted nervously, Master made us pass them. This we did as quickly as we could, for we horses, like some human beings, are afraid of the dead.

On some of the fence-posts, oven-birds had built their curious nests, which looked just like huge ostrich eggs made of clay. They have tiny entrances, cleverly built in the shape of spirals, which prevent the cold winds from blowing into the cosy interiors of the nests. Sometimes prairie-owls screeched at us as we passed them, turning their heads round till they faced backwards, which made them look very comical. Again, *tero-tero* birds would make a terrible fuss as we disturbed them. They have very shrill, piercing voices and are about the size of sea-gulls. Their colour is grey and black, they have long legs and

37

funny little feathers on their heads, like pee-wees.

When an enemy prowls over the prairie, and the *tero-teros* have young ones in a nest—which they build on the ground— they sneak away from it, and when they are some distance away they begin to call, "Tero-tero-tero!" all the time pretending that their nest is where they are making all the fuss. They fly up into the air and swoop past the enemy, and then return to the place where they want him to believe their young ones are. They squat on the ground as if protecting their offspring with spreading wings, suddenly to rise into the air again, all the time uttering their shrill "tero-tero-tero"! This very often attracts the would-be murderer of the young *tero-teros,* but when he goes to the spot where he expects to find them he can nose around for a long time, and till he's sick of it. He'll find no nest and no young birds, for the cunning *tero-tero* parents have made a fool of another enemy!

For four days we trotted towards the north. At night we were put into corrals where we were fed, and when the first rays of the rising sun shot over the pampas we were already on our way again. Sometimes we tried to turn back, but it was no use —Master wouldn't let us, so we had to go where he guided us.

We passed through several villages and small towns, and on the fourth day we came to a place where there were so many, and such big houses, that we were frightened. We made such a fuss that Master could hardly hold us, and when we struggled too much in our terror at the things we saw, he dismounted and went afoot, leading us along as best he could.

The city we had reached is called Buenos Aires, and is the capital of the Argentine Republic. If I tried to tell you about all the strange and terrifying things we saw there, I'd never finish. Now I know all about them, for during the years that followed I learnt a lot, and now these things no longer frighten me.

Master led us through streets where a regular stream of cars, wagons and carts was moving along. We reared up and snorted, and when we tried to run away we were held back. After a while we lost all sense of direction, but as Master didn't seem to be afraid, we huddled against him and followed wherever he went.

Just imagine how we felt; for we had never seen so many houses and heard such a din! The motor-cars growled, shrieked and roared, and the trams and buses made noises like thunder. We thought that all these things were monsters which were about to pounce on us. I used to think that pumas made the loudest and most blood-curdling noises in the world, but when I heard the din in this city I thought I would die.

Presently another man joined us, and when Master handed him the lead-rope with which I was tied, this stranger led me, whilst Mancha nervously pranced along in front, carefully held by Master. Crowds of people hurried along these streets, some riding on queer things they call bicycles and motor-bicycles. We didn't mind when people stopped to look at us, but when some came too near, and even tried to touch us, we made ready to defend ourselves.

I remember a very funny thing that happened to Mancha in the middle of this city. Of course, at the time I didn't think it was a bit funny, but now, being a tame horse, and getting on in years, I can't help laughing when I remember it.

Mancha was prancing along when a big truck, loaded with cases full of bottles, came rattling towards us. The sight of all these bottles—like hundreds of shiny eyes—scared him so much that he stopped and snorted loudly. As the truck came nearer, Mancha started going backwards, and although Master did his best to stop him, my pal was too strong for him. Just then an Italian fruit-vendor passed with a hand-cart full of fruit, and when Mancha's tail-end bumped into it he got such a fright that he let fly with both hind-legs. The old hand-cart went flying into the air as if a bomb had exploded under it, and the fruit, oranges, peaches, apples, pears, grapes, bananas and melons, scattered all over like hail. I wish you had been there to see the poor Italian! First of all he ran away as if he were being chased by a swarm of hornets, and then he started to wave his arms about until he looked like a crazy ostrich flapping his wings. I had heard men talk and yell before, but once that Italian was wound up he jabbered like dozens of fowls when a fox prowls around their coop; and I can't help feeling that it's just as well that I couldn't understand what he said.

Presently a crowd collected, and then there was a terrible fuss till a policeman elbowed his way through the spectators who had stopped to see the fun. Mancha and I were so nervous that we pranced about and reared up, several men having to use all their strength to hold us. After a while Master gave the Italian some coins, and as we walked away I could still see the fruit-vendor waving about his arms and occasionally stoop down to pick up some of his precious fruit.

Mancha relates how he and his pal found out what a stable is

AFTER a long and terrifying walk through busy streets, we finally came to an open space where there was a huge house with a big door. To my amazement I saw several horses and riders come out of that door, which looked like the entrance to a big cave I used to know in Patagonia. Caves have always frightened me, for I know that some of our deadly enemies live in them.

When Master led me straight towards that big door, I propped and snorted, for I was afraid of that dusky cave into which he wanted me to go. After a long struggle against several other men who had come to help Master, I was forced to enter the mysterious cave which, I found out later, was a stable where men sometimes keep their horses. To my surprise I saw quite a number who eyed us with curiosity as we passed their stalls and boxes. When I had calmed down I had a good look round and sniffed the air. Gato was tied near me, and further along there were other horses who were eating or having a sleep.

When I looked down, I noticed that I was standing on lovely golden-coloured straw. At the time I didn't know that this was put there by grooms, and was intended to be my bed, for we wild horses in Patagonia don't know such luxuries. First of all I sniffed the straw suspiciously, and I noticed that Gato was doing the same. After a short conversation with him we decided to taste it; and finding that it was quite good, we started to gobble it up. The men who were watching us from behind laughed boisterously, and a big hunter who was tied near me turned his proud head away in disgust.

Goodness, what a lot we had to learn before we were fit to be in the society of cultured and refined horses! Still, somehow we managed, but we never really liked it, for we much prefer to be natural. After all, good manners don't make a good horse.

Every day we learnt something new in that stable, and as nobody ever hurt us, we no longer felt strange, but began to take an interest in the things that were going on in the place. We were taught to stand still whilst being washed and brushed. Just think; washed and brushed! Why? When we were out in the wilds the rain did it for us, and if we felt like it, we had a dip in a lagoon or in a river, and when we came out of the water, the sun and wind did the drying and brushing for us.

In that stable we also had to learn that bran, oats and corn are good to eat. At first we didn't care for them, but after a few days, when we found out that they were good, we gobbled them up like the other horses did.

One day we were taken into a blacksmith's shop; and you can imagine what kind of a Patagonian war-dance we led the men until they finally managed to nail shoes on us. I still feel funny in the stomach when I remember how frightened I was of the fire, and of the red-hot shoe which was put to one of my hoofs before fitting it on. I struggled and fought for several hours, but what with ropes and men holding me I had to give in, and when I was taken back to the stable I had an iron shoe on each foot.

Later on, when I got to know what these shoes are tacked on for, I didn't mind standing still and lifting my legs, but you can imagine that I didn't like it for the first few times. Every day Master came to see us. Usually he led us outside into a big fenced-off circle where he mounted and made us trot or canter round and round. Sometimes he took us into a public park to show and teach us things, but when he did this he only took one at a time, for even with one alone he had enough trouble to keep him busy.

I remember when he showed me the first train. As the engine came hissing and snorting towards me, I got such a fright that I raced away as if a thousand pumas were after me. That engine scared me so much that I didn't even notice all the motor-cars and other monsters. I simply raced past them and along a road, as fast as I could. Once I lost my footing on the slippery surface and fell, but in a jiffy I was up again and fleeing for dear life. Fortunately Master didn't fall off, or else he might have been hurt. He tried hard to stop me by pulling at the bridle, but I raced on and on until a mounted policeman came dashing along. The presence of another horse soon inspired me with a feeling of safety, and gradually I slowed down, and finally stopped. I was exhausted and trembling with fear, and even when I was back in the stable with my pal Gato, the perspiration still rolled off me in streams.

With all the excitement of seeing new things every day, we hadn't even time to be sad, but during the nights, when we heard the other horses munch their fodder, we often remembered our dear herd in Patagonia and our friends and relations in the big field in the pampas.

Tied as we were, we could not mix with the other horses, but perhaps it was just as well, for they were not of our kind, and wouldn't have understood us. After all, Gato and I are mustangs and all the other horses in the stable were quite different. They were much taller, and perhaps, better-looking than we are, and they only seemed to be interested in their fodder, which they gobbled up by the bucketful. They were much too haughty and spoilt to eat the straw of their bedding, and I often wonder what would happen to such horses if they had to pass a winter in Patagonia.

Every day their masters came to ride them. What funny flat saddles they used, and what swanky clothes they wore! When I looked at some of these riders, and saw the way they sat on their long-legged horses, I wondered what they would look like if they tried to ride a wild mustang.

STORY TWELVE

*Gato's account of a trick Mancha played on Master; and
how they started out on a long, long trail*

MANCHA was talking about riders and the clothes some of them
wear. This reminds me of something that happened outside the
stable in Buenos Aires.

Every day some of these elegantly-dressed people came to
look at us. They used to stand behind our stalls for hours, and
made remarks about us. Some of the men stroked their
moustaches and shook their heads, whilst pointing at our legs
and other parts of our bodies with their little riding-whips. I
really believe they were pretending to know a lot about us.
Master didn't seem to take much notice of them, and he treated
them much in the same way as we did the other horses in the
stable.

One morning, we had an awful shock when Master arrived.
At first we thought it was not he who came up to us, and we
were just about to lift a warning hoof when we recognised his
smell. He was dressed like the city riders—no wonder we didn't
know him at first!

He spoke to us for a while and stroked our necks, and when
he had put the saddle on Mancha he led the two of us outside.

I've told you before that Mancha used to be a bad boy when
he was young. Well, that morning he happened to be in one
of his boisterous moods, and was a very naughty boy.

45

First he looked at Master's spotless riding-breeches and then at me, giving a saucy wink. If Master had been wise he would have noticed this, and would have taken good care to tighten the girth more firmly.

However, he seemed to be very pleased with himself that morning, and just went ahead straightening his neck-tie and humming a tune.

Just before he mounted, Mancha gave me another meaning wink, but even this didn't rouse Master's suspicions. He leapt into the saddle with confidence, but before you could say "hoof," Mancha started to buck and plunge so hard that he raised a cloud of dust. He squealed with joy when the saddle began to turn, and realising that he was winning the game, he tried every one of his old Patagonian tricks.

Poor Master! When he found out that he hadn't tightened the girth enough, it was too late; and just as he tried to jump off, naughty old Mancha arched his back like a cat, and gave a buck which sent Master, spotless riding-breeches, new neck-tie and all, high into the air. He flew to the other side of the fence, where he landed with a splash in a pool of mud and water! Poor Master! Although I snorted with mirth, I couldn't help feeling sorry for him. You should have seen him when he got up! What had been swanky riding-breeches and a lovely neck-tie were now a mass of mud, and Master looked like a piebald mustang I used to know in the wilds!

During the next few days I noticed that Master was making preparations for something, for he brought a pack-saddle, blankets, and all sorts of instruments. Mancha and I put our heads together and nickered about the mystery of these things.

Very early one morning Master arrived at the stables. He brought with him all sorts of things: clothes, guns, ammunition, and many other articles we didn't know, and on a leash he led a big Alsatian dog. After he had carefully packed some of these things into his saddle-bags he took us out of our stalls and started to saddle up.

When his pampas saddle—with all its sheep-skins—was fixed on me, he went over to put the pack-saddle on Mancha. Holy cats of Egypt! What a show it was! All this pack and saddle-bag business was new to Mancha, who tried his best to kick and buck the things off before they were strapped on. The stable-boys shouted and used bad language, and Master worked till he was red and blue in the face. At last, however, Mancha had to give in; and when I saw him with all the pack on his back, I couldn't help smiling, for he looked so funny and disgusted.

When all was ready, Master mounted on me, and, taking Mancha by the lead-rope, guided us out into the street.

Before we had gone far, newspaper-men and Press-photographers came to speak to him. It was no easy matter to make Mancha stand still, but when he finally did for a brief moment, the men pointed their cameras at us, whereupon they departed smiling. I couldn't see the joke, and I'm sure Mancha wasn't in the best of moods with all this nasty pack on him.

I guessed that we were going far away, and I hoped it would be towards the south. However, I was disappointed, for again our noses were made to point north.

By this time we were more or less used to houses and motor-cars, so we trotted along quickly and without making much fuss. Of course, we had a few scares before we reached the outskirts of the city, for there were still many things we didn't know.

As soon as we were out of the city, the roads were no longer paved, and as it had started to rain, we had to wade through puddles and mud which were often so deep that we could only plod along very slowly. The dog still followed us, and I must admit that I did not like his looks. Out in the pampas I had seen several wild dogs which we treated as dangerous enemies, for every now and again a foal was eaten by them. Master's dog waded through the mud behind us, and although we warned him several times not to come too near, he didn't seem to care. We hadn't gone very far when, all of a sudden, he appeared close to Mancha, who got such a fright that he kicked with both hind-legs. The next thing I saw was the dog flying through the air and falling into the ditch, where he lay as dead in the mud and water.

Master seemed to be very worried, for, as soon as he had tied us to the fence which ran along the road, he went to look at the dog. To my surprise he picked him up and carried him for some distance and then laid him down again. After that he returned to us and led us ahead, and then went back to pick up the dog. This he did several times till we came to a better road over which motor-cars travelled. We couldn't understand why Master bothered about an animal as dangerous as a dog, but you must remember that we didn't know then that dogs can be such good friends with men, and even with us horses.

What a job Master had! As he waded through the soft mud the rain poured down in buckets, and what with carrying the heavy dog and pulling us through the mire, he perspired like a mustang after bucking.

After a while a car stopped, and the two men who were in it took the dog with them. When, nearly three years later, we returned home, we found out that Mancha had broken one of the poor dog's bones, but by the time we came back he had recovered. To-day the three of us are the best of friends, and both Mancha and I enjoy it when the dog comes to visit us.

Mancha's impressions about the first stages of the long journey

THE first day of our journey was most unpleasant, to say the least. The pack-saddle tickled me, and every now and again I saw something that frightened me. To make things worse, it rained hard, and the road was so muddy that we sank in deep with every step.

In the evening Master took us into the yard of a country police-station where he took off our saddles, whereupon he went away to fetch us some fodder. After about an hour he returned with a huge bale of hay on his back, and soon we were too busy to take notice of several men who peeped at us from cells with small and heavily-barred windows. During the night several tramps and drunken rascals were brought in, and what with the noise and fuss these men made we didn't get much of a rest.

Before daybreak Master appeared, and after a lot of trouble he managed to put the saddle on me. Goodness, how all those straps and things tickled! Gato was made to carry the pack, and it was my turn to carry Master. I was in a very bad temper that morning, so I bucked a little, but when I found that it only tired me, I gave in and went where Master guided me.

Again we were made to go north; further and further away from home. After the first few days' travelling, one day was like another. We trotted over a vast prairie which looked like a limitless sea of grass. We followed a wide track which was fenced in on both sides, the posts and wires stretching in two dead straight lines until they were lost from view at the horizon. Heavy rains continued to pour down every day, and in many places the track was so soft that it was hard work to plod through the mud and water. We were so bored that we didn't even look at the prairie-owls who sat on fence-posts screeching at us. When we occasionally saw horses in the distance we no longer called them, for by this time we knew that we were in a strange land where we had no friends.

By degrees we got to know Master so well that we began to like him, and as time went on our liking grew into love and affection.

Gato and I took it in turns to carry Master, the one with the pack following behind.

On and on we jogged. Sometimes we spent the night in a ranch, but when we camped out in uninhabited parts Master slept on the ground near us. If a stranger came near, we heard or scented him long before he saw us, and on such occasions we snorted to wake up Master, but if he slept so heavily that he didn't hear us, we pushed our noses against him.

In spite of the many hardships we endured on our long journey, we had some joys and many good laughs. Of course, in most cases, when something funny happened, we only saw the joke afterwards, and at the time didn't think it a bit amusing, excepting when it happened to another member of our small expedition. I remember when we were slowly crossing the Argentine pampas, Mancha and I had a hearty laugh at Master's expense.

E

We had been travelling since long before daybreak when we came to a nice *arroyo,* as they call a brook in South America. As it was just about noon, and some good grass grew near there, Master unsaddled and turned us loose that we might roll, drink and graze whilst he made himself a can of coffee and had something to eat. Very often he had a snooze, and as we grazed somewhere near, we used to listen to his snoring.

The day we stopped at that *arroyo* it happened to be very hot, and as Master seemed to be tired, he soon was fast asleep, his head resting on the saddle, which was his usual pillow.

Whilst we were quietly grazing, there was a rustle in the grass, and presently I saw a lovely skunk. He had a nice bushy tail and two white stripes down his glossy black coat, and was probably on his way towards the *arroyo* to quench his thirst. As it happened, Mr. Skunk went straight towards Master, who, whilst he was dozing, had been bothered by a fly which insisted on settling on the tip of his nose. Just as the skunk was near, Master suddenly raised his arm to flick away the aggravating fly, at the same time making a hissing noise as he blew air at the tantalising insect. I wish you had been there to see the jump that the startled skunk gave, and I wish you had seen what happened immediately after that.

Before Master had finished making his hissing noise, our unexpected black and white visitor lifted his tail and squirted some of his awful smelling liquid at him.

I've often seen Master move quickly, but on that occasion he leapt to his feet like a Jack-in-the-box, giving us a fright. I don't think he'll ever wake up quicker than he did that afternoon. Goodness, how he ran, choked and coughed! One might have thought a thistle had got stuck in his throat. First of all he just dashed about in a circle, and when he could see again through his watering eyes, he made a straight rush for the *arroyo* and dived in with a splash—for all the world like a gigantic frog! The two of us looked on and laughed till our ribs ached, and when Mr. Skunk saw that there would be no more trouble, he strolled away as if nothing had happened.

After a while Master came out of the stream and took off all his clothes, and having found the soap in the pack, started to wash and scrub himself. When this was done he rinsed his clothes, in vain attempts to rid them of the overpowering smell. Mr. Skunk had done us a good turn, for, instead of saddling up again, Master unrolled his blankets and arranged the saddles on the ground; and we rightly guessed that there would be no more travelling for us that day.

All that afternoon and evening Master washed his clothes, and although he kept on muttering things to himself, we didn't listen, for we were much too busy grazing and chuckling to ourselves.

Thank you, Mr. Skunk! We shall never forget that *arroyo* in the pampas, and the lovely feed we had there, not to mention the hearty laugh!

One evening, after a long day's plodding through water and mud, we arrived at a humble little ranch-house. Torrential rains had beaten down on us all day, and to make things even more unpleasant, a strong wind began to blow as an early dusk fell on the dreary plains.

As we approached the ranch-house, a number of barking and snarling dogs came dashing towards us, but Master took no notice, and made us go on. When we were near the house he clapped his hands and called "Ave Maria!"—the customary manner for travellers to announce their arrival in the Argentine pampas. No stranger ever gets off his horse until he is invited to do so. Even the dogs seem to know this, for they keep on barking and threatening until their master calls them away.

Presently, several men and women appeared at the door, and although Master was a stranger to them, they politely asked him to dismount, and invited him to enter into the hut. These kind people even helped him to unsaddle us, and when we had been turned loose, they and Master went into the house, where a big fire roared up the chimney.

We grazed for a while, but it continued to rain in torrents, and the wind was so cold that we preferred to take shelter behind the walls of the house. Occasionally, when we heard Master's voice, we peeped in through the door to see what he was doing.

The people inside had obviously just finished a meal, for the spear—on which they had roasted a side of sheep—was still stuck in the mud floor near the fire. The dogs were gnawing bones which had been thrown to them, while the men were sitting close to the fire in a semi-circle. To light their cigarettes, the cowboys picked up burning cinders with the points of their large knives. Some were sitting on little stools which were made of two hip-bones of cows, cleverly tied together with strips of raw hide and covered with the skins of calves. Other men and women squatted on the sun-bleached skulls of horses, which are often used as stools among the more primitive people in the pampas.

Several children cuddled up against their mothers, their black eyes gleaming as they looked at the fire over which hung a large kettle which hummed and chirruped as the water was beginning to boil.

Presently one of the gauchos (Argentine cowboys) poured some of the hot water into a little gourd which was filled with the *maté* tea you have already heard about, and when the *bombilla*, or metal tube, had been stuck into it, the gourd was handed round, and everybody sucked a little of the green tea.

For a long time nobody spoke, and only the crackling of burning logs and the crunching noise of dogs gnawing bones, broke the silence. When a particularly strong blast of wind roared down the big chimney, sending a mass of whirling sparks and smoke into the room, it sounded just like the snort of a wild horse.

On such occasions a grizzly old cowboy shook his mop of long white hair, and pointing a horny finger at the darkness beyond the open door, said: "The snorting of the *Bragado*."

From where we were watching and listening, we heard Master ask the old man to tell the story of the *Bragado*. Finally, when the old man had seated himself in a more comfortable position, he started to speak very slowly, and in a deep bass voice.

"The Lagoon Bragado," he began, "is still infested with wild ducks, flamingoes and many other varieties of wild birds; very much as it was over a hundred years ago, when my story opens.

" 'Bragado' is the name of a beautiful stallion who was first seen by two trappers who were on their way to a distant store. In those days the pampas were quite uninhabited, and only a few settlements snuggled against the mountains to the far south-east. These settlements were fortified so as to make them safe from attacking Indians and fierce bands of outlaws, who were a great danger in those days.

"Here and there the prairieland was covered with patches of thorny bush, and only an occasional *ombú* tree broke the monotony of the seemingly endless plain.

"The two trappers who first sighted the 'Bragado' were earning money by the sale of hides and skins. One day, whilst they were creeping along a brook, stalking some ostriches, they beheld a sight which made them stop as if spellbound. On a hill, like a sentry on guard, stood a stallion, a magnificent, blood-red beast with white-blotched flanks. He was nervously quirking his ears as if to locate by some sound the place in which his instinct told him were enemies. On the lower ground about him was his herd, over which the stallion towered like the statue of a horse on a pedestal—motionless save for his twitching ears and slightly quivering, wide-open nostrils.

"When the two trappers arrived at the next settlement they told everybody about the beautiful stallion they had seen, and soon the name of the 'Bragado' became famous. So many were the extraordinary tales that were told about him that expeditions were being organised to go in search of him. However, in spite of all these efforts to capture the animal, the 'Bragado' always escaped easily, only to appear again in some other part.

"On several occasions he even allowed his would-be captors to come quite close before whirling round and uttering the call that brought his herd to heel and sent it off like a cloud of mist before the wind. Sometimes, in a spirit of mockery, the 'Bragado' had even galloped through the advancing line of cowboys, and in a cunning manner dodged the lassoes which were thrown at him.

"Soon the fame of the stallion reached the distant cities, and a wealthy trader decided to organise an expedition and send it into the pampas in search of the 'Bragado.'

"Two hundred men, some hired and others volunteers seeking adventure and glory, joined together. Covered wagons and provisions were bought, and for defence against Indians every man was armed with a rifle or some other weapon. Slowly the wagon train wound out of the city and was soon lost from sight on the horizon.

"The expedition had been on its way for several weeks, when, one evening, as the men were sitting about the camp preparing food, some scouts came back with the report that they had sighted the famous stallion. All the gauchos rushed to saddle their mounts, and soon they were advancing on their gallant prize. Riding in fan-formation they had planned to entrap the horse between themselves and a high, precipitous riverbank.

"The attack was so sudden and cleverly carried out that the 'Bragado' was separated from his troop. The dodging of men was no new thing to him, but this time every possible avenue of escape was cut off by the advancing riders, who were swinging their lassoes and *boleadoras*, a dangerous weapon the stallion had long ago learned to fear. As an attempt to break through the advancing line of enemies was impossible, he climbed up to the highest rock that projected above the river. Murmurs of admiration and calls of triumph escaped the cowboys as they realised the animal was at last securely trapped.

"He looked beautiful now, pawing and snorting, his body showing to full advantage with the setting sun behind him. The cool evening breeze played with his mane and flowing tail, and as if admitting defeat he tossed flecks of foam into the air.

"For a few seconds he stood at bay, and then, uttering a shrill neigh of defiance, he sprang into space and his beautiful body hurtled downward into the river, sinking immediately from sight; never to reappear.

"Silently the men returned to their camp near the lagoon, where later a village was founded. With the passing of years this village grew into a small town, its neat houses standing as a monument to the 'Bragado,' who, like many men, preferred death to bondage."

. . . .

After we had travelled over the prairies for many long days, the country began to change. The sun became hotter and hotter, and the ground was very sandy and dusty. Here there were no more fences, and in many places it was difficult to see the track. Vast stretches of the country were covered with a mass of white salty crystals, which made the place look as if it had snowed. Here and there grew huge cactus plants, some being as big as chestnut-trees—forty to sixty feet in height.

In the day-time it was terribly hot, and when we had our midday rest there was nothing to eat, except a few tufts of coarse salty grass. Sometimes Master cut the long and sharp thorns off cactus plants with a big knife, and chopped the thick bulgy leaves into slices which he gave us to eat. At first we were not keen on this new fodder, but when we tasted it and found that it was quite sweet and good, we ate every scrap Master prepared for us.

In this region we saw only two or three human beings, and very few animals, excepting lizards and an occasional snake. Some of these lizards were very big and beautiful, and as we approached them they waved one fore-paw as if beckoning to us to come nearer. Early in the morning and towards evening, flocks of little green parrots flew about, screeching loudly, but during the heat of the day they slept in shady spots among the cactus plants or in their big nests, in which several families live.

At night foxes prowled about, and owls flew silently above our heads. How I hated the mournful hooting of these birds, whose eyes sometimes stared at us like two bright yellow disks.

We were glad when we came out of this desolation of cactus plants and sand, for fodder had been scarce, and we had gone thirsty for hours till we found water, which was warm and tasted of salt.

Master was lucky to have us with him, for more than once when we were so thirsty that our tongues began to swell and prick as if pins were being stuck into them, we showed him the way to water-holes he would never have found without us. Men may be intelligent, but in some ways we horses are cleverer than you are. We can smell water long before we see it, and, moreover, we never lose our way.

On one occasion it was just as well that Master didn't interfere with us when we showed him the way to a water-hole, or else he might not be alive to-day. This is how it happened.

We had travelled for many hours, and the sun was so hot that it burned through my hide. Master, too, must have felt the heat, for he was unusually silent. As a rule, he chatted with us, and although we couldn't understand all he said, we liked to listen to his voice.

The region through which we were jogging was a desert where nothing grew but here and there a few shrubs and solitary cactus plants. Every time we came to a hollow, I noticed that Master looked for something, and I soon guessed that it was water he wanted. "How stupid!" I thought to myself. "Fancy looking for water with the eyes!"

For a long time we continued; and I was beginning to feel quite bad with the terrible thirst that tormented me. Suddenly a lovely smell of water reached my nostrils, and I sharply turned to the left where it came from.

Master seemed annoyed with me for having changed our course, but in spite of his efforts to make me go his way, I refused. Trying to make him understand that I was leading him to water, I raised my head, pricked up my ears and sniffed the air.

It was lucky for the three of us that Master guessed what I wanted to tell him, for as soon as he gave me my head, I took him straight to a hole where we found precious water.

After this, whenever we were in difficulties, Master always left the finding of water-holes to us.

STORY FOURTEEN

In which Gato continues the narrative, telling about
the next stages of the journey into Bolivia

WHEN I was young I never guessed that the world is so big, and
I didn't know that so many strange people and animals live in it.
If you want to get a good idea of the distance Mancha and I
have travelled, just look at the map on page 131 and see where
our hoofs have trodden. For thousands and thousands of miles
we went north from Patagonia. We crossed the whole of South
and Central America, and then jogged through Mexico, and from
there trotted on to Washington in the United States of America.
Sometimes we travelled through huge prairies, then we plodded
through tropical swamps, or we climbed up giddy mountain-
sides till we came to regions of eternal snows, high above the
clouds. Again, we fought our way through wide rivers and
raging mountain streams, most of which had no bridges; and
therefore had to be crossed by swimming. Some of the tropical
waters were full of alligators and crocodiles; and we were lucky
that no electric eels touched us, and that we were not stung by
rays, whose poison can even kill a horse.

Electric eels live in some of the slow-flowing streams and
rivers in the hot parts of South America. They are about four
feet long and black, and as thick as a man's arm. Their bodies
are like electric batteries, for they are filled with enough
electricity to stun a horse if they touch any part of his body.

61

Before entering some rivers and streams, Master had to look us over very carefully to make quite sure that we had no cuts or scratches anywhere, for if the cannibal fishes—who infest these waters—smell blood, they tear their victims to pieces in a few moments. These cannibal fishes are called *carribes* or *pirañas*.

We encountered many other perils on the way, but you will hear about them later.

What strange people we saw in some places! We lived among Indians who went about practically naked; and we even saw some who painted their bodies and faces.

Now I must go back to where Mancha left off, and tell you what happened when we left the cactus forests behind us and came to much nicer country where there was plenty of good grass and water.

Whilst we were trotting over an open stretch of grassland in the forest region in the north of the Argentine, we had a very exciting adventure.

I was carrying Master, who seemed to be half asleep, when the smell of an enemy I dreaded came to my keen nostrils. In a flash I turned and tried to flee in the opposite direction, but before I had gone ten yards, Master stopped me, and, much against my will, turned me round again. However, in spite of all his efforts to make me go ahead, I refused to make another step forward, and as he didn't seem to realise that a puma lay hidden somewhere ahead of us, I snorted and reared up, trying to make Master understand that I had scented danger. When he finally guessed that something was wrong, he dismounted, and, having tied the two of us to a tree, went to investigate.

He hadn't gone far when I heard a warning snarl which made me tremble with fear.

Presently, Master came running back to us, and having un-strapped his rifle—which was always on top of the pack—he slowly advanced towards the place where the puma lay hidden. At the time we didn't know what a rifle is used for, and we had often wondered what this strange stick on the pack might be.

Step by step Master advanced through the dry grass, whilst the two of us watched with horror, expecting him to be killed at any moment. After a while—which seemed like a whole day—he stopped and slowly raised the rifle to his shoulder.

With heads held high, we both looked on, our nostrils wide open so as not to miss the faintest smell which might come our way.

Suddenly a flash of fire came out of the muzzle of the rifle, and at the same instant there was a noise like a thunderbolt. I really don't remember what happened after, for the fright I got was so great and sudden that I can't tell you what I did. In trying to run away I got such a violent tug on my neck that I fell, and when I managed to scramble to my feet I fought madly to tear myself loose.

After a while I heard Master's voice, and when I could see clearly again I saw him standing near me. Having calmed down a little, I looked around me and saw Mancha who was still tied to a tree near-by, and I noticed that he was every bit as scared as I was.

Master spoke to us and stroked our necks, and, as soon as we were less nervous, he went over to the place where the puma had been hiding in the grass. Only when we realised that our enemy was dead, could we be persuaded to proceed on our way, but, for a long time after that, we were on the look-out for a sudden attack.

Later on Master taught us not to fear his fire-arms. After a few weeks we got so used to the deafening noise they made that we took but very little notice when he shot birds and animals, which were often his only food.

Every day we travelled far, until, after many long journeys, we saw mountains ahead of us. We were in very wild country now. There were no roads, and the few villages we came to were small and dirty. The people we saw there were much darker than those in Buenos Aires; in fact, most of them looked like Indians.

The country was getting very mountainous, and as not even trails existed there, we were obliged to travel along the dry river-beds. Slowly we penetrated further and further into the mountains. Sometimes we were shut in by high walls of rock, which rose straight up into the sky.

It was just as well that we had arrived during the dry season, for if we had been caught in one of these valleys when it rains in the high regions, and the wild waters come thundering and seething down the deep gorges, we would have been drowned like rats.

When we had crossed the whole of the Argentine we came to a country called Bolivia. Every now and again Indians with their troops of laden llamas passed us.

The first time I saw llamas I was terrified, but when Master made me understand that they are quite harmless, I plucked up courage and looked at them with curiosity. How strange they look with those long, upright necks and woolly coats! Very soon we got so used to seeing llamas that we took practically no more notice of them. Before I go on with my story I must tell you something funny about them.

You know that to defend himself, a horse kicks, a cat scratches, a dog bites, and a skunk makes a terrible smell. In fact, most animals have some kind of defence; but, as far as I know, llamas have no way of defending themselves, for they neither bite nor kick, nor do they scratch. However, they have a very nasty and most unpleasant habit. They spit! Yes, when they are annoyed they—spit!

Sometimes when we passed a troop of these llamas on a narrow mountain trail where animals and men have to walk in single file, it was very unpleasant if they didn't like the looks of Master. If the first llama made up its mind to spit, all the others which followed behind did the same; and you can guess what sort of a mess Master was in when a troop of llamas had passed him!

Travelling became more and more difficult as we advanced into the network of mountains. Sometimes we slowly picked our way through stony river-beds, where we struggled ahead for hours, stumbling over rocks and stones.

I have never seen anything more imposing and dreary than these enormous and deep valleys. There wasn't a trace of animals, and for days we saw nothing green, excepting here and there a cactus plant. Icy winds swept down from the snow-capped mountains ahead of us, and where these winds struck some rocks they produced a mournful, booming sound, which, together with the clattering of our hoofs, were the only noises to break the mysterious silence.

Sometimes we came to rivers we couldn't cross, and so we were forced to follow Indian foot-trails which led us up steep mountain-sides and along giddy precipices. In such places we had to be very careful and watch every step we took, for a slip or a careless movement would have meant certain death.

Soon we had so much confidence in Master that we went wherever he guided us. When we came to a steep incline, he always went afoot to make it easier for us, and we didn't mind it a bit when he caught hold of our tails to be pulled along. He was always very careful with the pack and saddle, and every now and again he stopped to see if they had slipped out of place. We got to understand each other so well that we could guess what Master wanted us to do; and by this time he understood us as easily as if we had been able to speak.

If one of us suddenly stopped, he guessed at once that something had gone wrong, and immediately came to investigate. Sometimes a stone had stuck in a hoof; the pack or the saddle had slipped, or, perhaps, one of us wanted to rest a minute.

We were now so high above sea-level that the air was very thin. The lack of air-pressure causes *mountain sickness*, which is very unpleasant, and sometimes even dangerous. The slightest physical effort makes the heart beat violently, and the sufferer vainly gasps for breath. Very often he bleeds from the nose and feels giddy, and, sometimes, even faints.

Master always told us to climb up these mountain-sides slowly, and whenever we stopped he never drove us on, but waited until we had recovered our breath.

At first we used to tremble and shiver with fear when we

looked down some of these giddy precipices, but we soon got so used to them that we didn't mind so much.

Once one of my feet got stuck between two rocks, and in the struggle to pull it out, I tore off the shoe. Master had often taught us to lift our legs; and to show us that he would do us no harm, he tapped the underneath part of our hoofs with a stone. Thanks to these lessons I didn't mind standing on three legs whilst he nailed on another shoe. He always carried several spare irons in the saddle-bag, and he also had a hammer and other tools which are necessary for shoeing a horse.

When I remembered the fight I put up when men tried to shoe me for the first time, I couldn't help smiling to myself. But, as you know, I wasn't tame at the time, and I thought the men wanted to do me some harm.

With all the lessons Master gave us, we quite enjoyed the fun when he said "*Left*" or "*Right*," and soon we got to know by sound which leg he wanted us to lift. You see, even a wild horse becomes tame and affectionate when he is taught with kindness and patience.

Mancha chats about Bolivia, high mountains and Indians

STRUGGLING along many enormous valleys and over cold, barren and wind-swept mountains, we had penetrated far into Bolivia.

Sometimes we met Indians who were on their way to distant towns and villages, where they exchange their woven goods and pottery for things they need in their mountain homes. The natives make these journeys once a year, setting out with their llamas and shaggy little donkeys when the dry season begins. Before they start they decorate the llamas with many coloured ribbons, which they attach to the plaited strands of hair, especially on the animals' heads and necks.

As a rule, the women and children stay at home and wait until the men return, but I've seen quite small children, and even women carrying babies, who trotted behind the laden llamas. At first I was amused to see the way these Indian women carried their *guauas* (babies), which are wrapped up in blankets and slung on the mothers' backs.

I don't think that it can be very good for the babies, and I wouldn't like to be in their place when they are being carried for miles and miles at a trot, often over very bad mountain trails.

All these Indians spoke languages I didn't understand. I could tell that Master had great difficulty when he wanted to ask the natives something, for he explained himself by moving his arms and hands, but usually he managed to obtain what he needed; food, water and shelter.

Often we travelled for several days without seeing anything green, for in some of the valleys—or *quebradas*, as they are called in Spanish—there is no earth, and therefore no plants can grow.

Before we came to such places, Master used to fill a sack with corn, and load it on top of the pack.

Here and there, when we came to a lonely stone hut where Indians lived, we were given a little straw, which is the only fodder their llamas and donkeys get.

These mountain Indians are very strange, but interesting people. They are always weaving cloth, which is done on a simple wooden framework on the ground. They use the wool of llamas and sheep, which is first of all twisted into thread. This is also done by hand, and with the help of a wooden top through which a stick is stuck. The bits of wool are attached to the upper end of this stick, and when it has been made to spin round by flicking it between the thumb and the middle finger, the wool is added on as the top and stick spin round—just like the tops children often play with.

Of course, it takes a long time to weave a big blanket, but Indians are very patient and work all day long.

They are also very clever at making pots which are fashioned in many shapes and painted in different colours and patterns.

It's surprising to see how industrious these people are, for in spite of the fact that the land in which they live is mostly barren, they have cultivations which are the result of sheer hard work. With great patience they build terraces on the mountain-sides, and when these are finished and have been fenced in with low stone walls, the men, women and children go long distances to fetch earth with which they fill these terraces. Sometimes soil is brought from far away, everybody filling as big a basket as they can carry on their backs.

To irrigate the tiny cultivations on the terraces, water is brought there through little canals, which are hewn out of the rocky sides of the mountains.

In the day-time it's usually very hot in the Bolivian mountains, but as soon as the sun sets it gets very cold. To protect themselves against these extremes of temperature, the natives wear warm clothes. The men use funny trousers which are slit at the sides—from the bottom up to the knees. At first I thought that these slits were just a fashion, but later I found out that they are really very useful.

You must have noticed the wide trousers sailors wear; and probably you know that they are purposely cut like that to make it easy to take them off with shoes on, or to roll them up over the knees when the decks have to be washed.

The slits in the Bolivian Indians' trousers are made for similar purposes, for when these hardy natives travel—which they always do afoot—they are often obliged to wade through water or mud. On reaching a bad place they take off their sandals, and, after having rolled up their trousers, they wade through.

Instead of overcoats, the men wear big square blankets, with slits in the middle, through which they stick their heads. Master used to wear one of these *ponchos* which, at night, served him as a cover.

The Indian women wear thick woollen skirts and blouses;

and in some regions, huge flat hats are part of the feminine attire. When an Indian lady greets a man, she takes off her hat; but the men never do this to women, for among these people it would be considered bad form and lack of manners.

About four hundred years ago, when the Spaniards first discovered South America, no sheep, dogs, chickens and donkeys were to be seen there; and, as Gato has already told you in Story Two, the Indians had never seen horses until white men invaded their lands.

As soon as the Spaniards realised that the newly discovered continent was rich, they brought domestic animals from Spain in their ships; and when the Indians first saw these creatures they were afraid of them.

On one occasion the natives watched chickens being let out of their cages, and when a cock flapped his wings and crowed, the Indians ran helter-skelter, for they thought that an animal which can make such a noise must be dangerous. And yet these same Indians weren't afraid of leopards and big snakes, nor did they fear bears and other fierce beasts!

However, they very soon got to know all the new animals which white men brought across the ocean on their ships, and now, four hundred years later, they use them much the same as you do; and they don't even remember that their forefathers were afraid when they first saw the domestic animals you all know and love.

The Indians are not the same everywhere, nor do they speak the same language. According to the climate, their dress varies a great deal, for where it's cold the natives wear warm clothes, and where it's hot they wear only very little, or nothing at all.

AIMARA INDIAN
BOLIVIA

As you must know, plants also vary a great deal, according to the climate in which they grow. In regions of perpetual ice and snow, there's no vegetation at all, and in places where it's not quite so cold, plants and trees have only thin leaves. The needles of fir-trees are really leaves; the frost can't wither them, and they grow even where it snows.

As we travelled towards the warmer regions, the leaves of plants got bigger and bigger, until we saw some which were as large as garden umbrellas.

If you took one of these big-leafed tropical plants and put it where it freezes, it would at once shrivel up and die, for the cold would freeze the juice with which it is filled, and thus kill it.

Some of the jungle Indians are very interesting, for they lead strange lives and often do extraordinary things.

Where it's hot they sleep in open huts—like shelters with big roofs to protect against the sun and rain. These roofs are usually made of dry palm-leaves or grass. The people sleep in hammocks or on beds which look rather like shelves made of sticks.

Many of the jungle Indians never work, for all they have to do to live is to go hunting and fishing. Most of the hunting is done with bows and arrows, or with spears; but in some parts the natives use blow-guns and poisoned darts.

I've seen quite a number of blow-guns, which are made with great skill and ingenuity.

First of all the Indians find a straight piece of hard wood, about six to eight feet in length. When it has been cut and dried, a very small hole is bored through it, from one end to the other. The walls of this hole must be very smooth, or else the dart would not pass through it. A blow-gun resembles a very long and thick pea-shooter, but, instead of peas, tiny darts are shot out of it. These are made of the tips of straight and tough thorns, about one inch in length, or of thin fish-bones which are sharpened to fine points. Very small and fluffy feathers are fixed on to the blunt ends of the darts, making them look just like the tiny projectiles for air-guns.

Before these small darts are pushed into the blow-gun, they are dipped into mysterious and deadly poisons, and then the hunter is ready to stalk his prey.

Creeping through the dense jungle, the Indian approaches an unsuspecting animal or bird, and when he is near enough, he puts the blow-gun to his mouth and sends out the tiny, silent messenger of death.

Shortly after the sharp point of the dart has embedded itself into the flesh of the victim, the poison begins to act, and soon the animal drops down dead.

In spite of the fact that poison has caused the animal's death, the meat can be eaten without the slightest danger.

During jungle wars these blow-guns are formidable weapons, for if an Indian hides in a tree, or among the dense vegetation, he can shoot the deadly darts without the enemy being aware of it until he feels a sting like a mosquito-bite.

For fighting, the tips of arrows are dipped in similar poisons, and if an enemy is even only slightly wounded he is sure to be killed by the poison.

Luckily, however, these Indians are fairly peaceful people, and only fight when their land is being invaded. After all, what right have white men to go into the territory which has belonged to those Indians for thousands of years? Wherever white men have gone they have taken the land from the natives, whom they killed without mercy for trying to defend their homes.

None of these jungle dwellers ever tried to do any harm to us; in fact, they were quite kind and brought us things to eat.

When fishing the Indians go out on the rivers or lagoons in canoes: just tree-trunks which have been hollowed out. At one end of these canoes they construct platforms with strong bamboo canes.

Probably you know that if a man stands well above the surface of water he can see much better what's in it than if he is low down. If you stand on a bridge and look down, you can often see the fish in the water, but if you look from a boat you can't see anything below the surface.

The Indian who stands up on the platform waits until he sees a big fish below him, and then he throws a spear at his prey.

The point of the spear is made of hard wood, which is barbed to make it grip when it has penetrated into the flesh. In some parts of South America the Indians shoot fish with their bows and arrows. Standing on one of the platforms I've just mentioned, or on a river-bank, they look out for a fish, and when the opportunity presents itself they take careful aim and shoot their arrows into the water. To these they attach a long piece of string, to the end of which is fixed an air-inflated bladder. If an arrow hits a fish, and the barbed point embeds itself in the flesh, the unfortunate victim leaps out of the water, or dives down to the bottom, making desperate efforts to rid itself of the arrow. As the fish struggles and swims away, the string plays itself out until the bladder is pulled into the water.

I suppose most of you have swum with bladders or "wings" to keep you afloat, so you can imagine what happens to the poor fish. Wherever he dashes, the bladder goes with him, and the Indians follow it in a canoe. Every time he rises to the surface, the men send off other arrows, until the victim dies.

The further we went into Bolivia the higher were the mountains we came to. They are all part of the Andes, which is the biggest mountain chain in the world, stretching from the north to the extreme south of the South American continent.

Sometimes we went along deep and narrow valleys, called *canyons*, or we zig-zagged up steep mountain-sides to cross over high passes where there was so little air that breathing became difficult.

Whilst digging among some ancient graves, Master had poisoned one of his hands. As we went on he got worse and worse, and after a few days his face and hands began to swell so much that the skin cracked. Both his hands were practically useless, and the poison even spread down to one of his legs. Soon he was unable to wear one of his riding-boots, being obliged to put on a sandal which he obtained from an Indian.

At last we came to a small settlement where a clever native herb doctor cured the invalid, who took some time to recover completely.

The last road we had seen was now hundreds of miles behind us, and we considered ourselves to be lucky when we jogged over a trail which most of you would call "frightful."

Before I go further with my story, I want to explain something about the Indians.

Has it ever struck you that it's strange that the natives of the Americas are called "Indians"?

Surely Indians must be the people who live in India; and the people who inhabit North and South America ought to be called "Americans."

Just in case you don't know why the natives of the Americas are called "Indians," I'll tell you how this came about.

In the year 1492, when Columbus crossed the Atlantic Ocean, on his ship called *Santa Maria,* he was really seeking a short cut from Spain to India. After a long sea-journey, when Columbus and his men sighted land, they thought they had arrived in India. Shortly after having landed, the Spanish sailors saw some Redskins; and thinking these people were natives of India, they called them "Indians."

A number of years later, when Columbus died, he didn't know that he had discovered a new continent, for he still thought he had merely found a short route to India.

When I tell you stories about South American Indians, I want you to remember that they aren't all alike. As a matter of fact, the difference between some of the Indians is greater than that between an Englishman and an Arab. In some parts of South America the natives are only light-brown in colour, whereas in other places they are quite dark. Besides their colour, they also vary in looks, for some have features which resemble those of white men. Many South American Indians look like Mongolians, and others have big, ugly mouths and thick, flat noses. Wherever we went the natives spoke different languages and dialects, and their clothes varied as much as their form of speech.

Some Indians, who live in hot parts, paint their bodies and faces, and, to adorn themselves, make cuts in their faces, bodies and limbs. These gashes are filled with paint, and once the wounds have healed, the colours remain there for good, like the tattoo savages—and even some white people—disfigure themselves with.

We were going ahead, further and further into the Bolivian mountains. The trails were terrible, and there was only little, or even nothing to eat. Sometimes we spent a whole day climbing up a steep mountain, or winding our way down a giddy footpath.

The Indians who live up in those mountain regions of Bolivia are quite unlike their cousins: the jungle-dwellers. They love music and dancing, and sometimes spend whole days beating their drums and playing huge flutes, made of bamboo-cane. On special occasions, some of the men dress up in bear-skins, and wear frightful masks while others disguise themselves as monkeys or devils. Some of the dancers wear huge hats, made of the bright feathers of tropical birds. These colourful hats are about as big as umbrellas, but, being made of split bamboo cane and feathers, they don't weigh much.

When these Indians dance they form a circle around the musicians, and hobble or hop about in single file, every now and again yelling as loudly as they can.

Very soon I got so used to seeing Indians dance, that—if I was lucky enough to have some straw or dry corn-stalks to eat— I just stodged away, and hardly bothered to watch the dancers.

One day Master gave us and the Indians a good laugh. He was watching one of these dances when one of his Indian friends made him a sign to join in the fun. Master hesitated for a while, and then suddenly rushed into the circle of dancers, and started to hop about like a crazy hen.

The disguised Indians—monkeys, devils and other hideous monsters—stopped and looked, but the musicians doubled their efforts, thumping their huge drums with all their might, and blowing the bamboo flutes till the veins on their necks stuck out like bits of cord.

I had seen Master in funny moods before, but what he did at that dance was so amusing that I stopped chewing a piece of corn-stalk I had in my mouth.

According to the rhythm of the music, he kicked his legs and twisted about as if horse-flies were biting him, and he threw about his arms, which reminded me of the incident in Buenos Aires when I upset the Italian fruit-vendor's hand-cart.

The Indians must have thought Master was a wonderful

dancer, for when they didn't laugh they watched with admiration, staring from under their horrid masks which made them look like apparitions in some strange nightmare.

When Master saw that his antics pleased and amused the natives, he started to turn cart-wheels and somersaults, and he even walked on his hands.

I was beginning to wonder if the old blood-poisoning had affected his brain when I happened to look at my pal Gato who was standing near me. He, too, must have been worried, for I saw him sadly shake his head.

The Indians were so pleased with Master's performance that they gave him things to eat and drink. A native—who was dressed up as a devil—ran away, soon to return with a big armful of corn-stalks which he deposited in front of us.

After that, whenever I was hungry, I always wished that we'd come to an Indian dance and that Master would again perform his funny tricks.

.   .   .   .

In many ways Indian children much resemble their white cousins, for when they have nothing else to do, they play and romp about.

Little girls often play with dolls, which are just made of wood or bits of wool. Even though these dolls are very ugly, and look nothing like small children, the Indian girls are very proud and fond of them. Many a time I've seen such dolls being carried about by little tots who slung them on their backs in blankets, or who cuddled them affectionately.

Since Indian children never go to school, you might think

they have a lot of time for play, but, as a matter of fact, this is not so, for even when they are very young they have to help their parents. Boys and girls assist with the weaving and making of thread, and if their parents have llamas or sheep, the children mind them from sunrise to sunset. When pottery is being made, the youngsters help to soften the clay, a task which is performed by hand, or by treading on the clay till it is soft and has no lumps or air-bubbles.

In the jungles, children learn to use bows and arrows when they are quite young, for it takes years of practice to become a good archer and a successful hunter.

Some youngsters love to play with beetles, frogs, harmless snakes, and similar live toys, but, speaking generally, Indians are kind to animals; and I've never seen them intentionally torment or ill-treat their pets.

In the hot regions the kids love to assemble near pools or streams, and when they bathe you can hear them shout and laugh, even though you're far away from them. Before they go into the water they must be very careful and make quite sure that no crocodiles or alligators are lurking there. The youngsters must never go to places against which their parents have warned them, or else they might get stung by rays, or be devoured by pirañas, besides running the risk of being caught in mud-holes which suck their victims down to certain death.

I've often seen Indian boys and girls who practised throwing stones with slings. This must be very difficult to do well, for once or twice Master tried his hand at it, but he was such a rotten shot that all the kids laughed.

The little Indian girls help their mothers to do the cooking, which is done in pots made of baked clay. A fire is made in a hole in the ground, and over this the pot is placed.

In most parts, fire-wood is so plentiful that one hasn't to go far to collect an armful. To start a fire, two bits of soft wood are rubbed together till they begin to smoulder, whereupon dry fibres are put near them, and fanned till they catch fire.

Although Indian children don't go to school, they have a great deal to learn, for hunting and fishing isn't at all easy; and to know the names of all the animals, and to understand their many strange ways, is a long study. By the time a native child has grown up, he or she knows most of the plants and trees. Some Indians are very good at preparing medicines and tonics from leaves, herbs and roots.

I remember an Indian who gave Master a thick piece of bamboo-cane which was filled with an ointment to keep off mosquitoes and other insects. This ointment was pink in colour and had a lovely scent of flowers. After a little of this stuff had been rubbed on us we weren't tormented by insects for at least two days. I was very sorry when there was no more of this wonderful ointment, for we were often plagued by thousands of mosquitoes and gnats which followed us like a small cloud.

.   .   .   .

Higher and higher we climbed into the Bolivian mountains. Sometimes Master slept in small Indian huts in which some stone blocks, or just the hard mud floor, served as bed. Gato and I used to wait outside, and when the icy night winds blew we sought shelter behind the hut.

After weeks of travelling, and often enduring hardships, we

came to the top of a mountain. Looking down towards the west we saw the huge table-land of Bolivia. As far as we could see it stretched like a golden plain, and in the distance a lake glittered with the rays of the setting sun.

On the following day we were down on that huge table-land, which is about 12,000 feet above the level of the ocean.

For several days we trotted over the monotonous sandy plain where water was very scarce. Sometimes we spent the night in miserable Indian villages, having to be content with an armful of straw or dry corn-stalks.

Some of the straw still had on it the ears, out of which the wheat had been threshed. The sharp whiskers often got stuck in the soft gums of our teeth, making our mouths very sore. When Master noticed this he put his hand into our mouths and removed the nasty things; and to cure us, wrapped a piece of cloth around the end of a stick. Having dipped it in water, he sprinkled salt on it, and then pushed the stick into our mouths, using it like a tooth-brush. The salt soon made our sore gums heal, and we were once more able to eat our coarse fodder without discomfort.

We horses are very fond of salt, which we like to lick as you would the icing off a cake. Wild horses and other animals must have salt, and will often go very far to find some.

By this time we were so used to travelling that I often felt as if I had done nothing else all my life. I could hardly believe that I had been afraid of Master not so very long ago; and Patagonia and my old friends seemed like memories of a strange dream. Now, as I jogged along, I only wondered where and when I would get my next drink of water and something to eat.

From the table-land, in the far distance, we could see the jagged peaks of mountain ranges which looked like the irregular teeth of a huge saw. After days of dull travelling towards the north, we passed near a beautiful mountain which was covered with glittering snow.

Having rested for a few days—in a town called La Paz, the capital of Bolivia—Master saddled up again; and within a few hours we were once more out in the wilds. Two days later we came to a lovely lake, high up in the mountains. The natives who live along the shores of this lake (Lake Titicaca) build very strange boats or canoes, which they call *balsas*. To build them, the Indians cut bulrushes, which they lay out in the sun to dry. Later these are tied together in the shape of long thick sausages, which, in their turn, are cleverly bound together and given the shape of a boat. However, the *balsas* are not hollow like the canoes or boats you know, for they are a solid mass of bulrushes, which, being lighter than water, float splendidly.

Sometimes the Indians make sails, but instead of cloth they split bulrushes and weave them into things that resemble fibre mats. To guide the *balsas*, long poles are used for steering.

Some of the Indians in these regions hate white men, and will not allow them to travel through their territory after dark. In the day-time they don't mind so much, but if a white man remains in their land after the sun has set they get very angry and sometimes even kill him.

The country along the banks of Lake Titicaca is very beautiful, but unfortunately we soon left its clear blue waters behind us and entered a big valley which led straight towards a very old Indian town called Cuzco.

Long before the Spaniards discovered America, the Indians had founded a great empire which extended for hundreds of miles along the Andes. The *Inca,* as the ruler of this empire was called, lived in palaces, the walls of which were lined with solid gold.

When the Spaniards arrived in their ships, the Inca went to greet them with a big army. However, before he knew what was happening there was thunder of shooting, and Spaniards came dashing up on horses. The Indians had never heard guns and rifles being fired, and they had never seen horses, which, as you already know, didn't exist in the Americas at that time.

The natives were terrified when the Spaniards, clad in shining armour, dashed into their ranks, swinging their swords and cutting men down left and right. The poor Indian soldiers only had lances and slings, which were of no use to them in the panic that ensued. The cunning Spaniards at once took the Inca prisoner, and when they realised how much treasure these Indians possessed, they asked for a huge ransom for their emperor. Although the price for his release was a big room full of gold, the Indians paid the huge ransom within a few days; but in spite of this the cruel white invaders killed the Inca and enslaved all his subjects.

.   .   .   .

We safely arrived at Cuzco—the ancient capital of the Inca Empire. This stately old town is situated up in the mountains of Peru, where many old walls and fortifications tell the sad tale of fallen glory and might.

Having rested for a few days we again set out, and headed straight for some high and wild mountains.

This story has been a long one, and as Gato had an exciting adventure on the next lap of our journey, I'll let him tell it himself.

STORY SIXTEEN

Gato talks about mountains, dangerous trails, an accident, vampire bats, and other things that happened until the little expedition arrived on the golden shores of the Pacific Ocean

WHEN we left the old town of Cuzco I guessed that new difficulties and hardships were in store for us, for I had observed Master overhaul the pack and fix new straps to the saddles. By this time I knew enough about equipment to guess that he was making preparations for climbing steep mountains.

One morning, after he had carefully put the saddles and pack on us, he mounted. Going at a lively trot we soon came to the end of the street which was paved with rough cobble-stones; and an hour later the old Indian town of Cuzco was out of sight. The pack felt rather heavy, suggesting that it was filled with food, which probably meant that we were going to wild parts where we would find but little to eat.

A stranger with two mules had joined us; and now, together, we headed for some mountains which rose sharply into the deep blue sky in the north.

The stranger seemed to know Master very well, but I'm sorry to say that neither I nor Mancha liked the company of the mules with their long ears, thin necks, and scraggy tails which hung down like two black snakes. Whenever they came near us we looked at them as fiercely as we could, and if this didn't make them go away, we lifted one hind-leg to show them what we'd

86

do if they took no notice and wouldn't keep at a respectful distance.

The presence of the strange man made us feel uncomfortable, for we were only used to Master, and we distrusted any other human being. Once or twice the stranger came too near Mancha, but after my pal had given him a good nip in the seat of his breeches, he took good care to keep away from us.

We had travelled about two or three days when we entered a net-work of terrible mountains and deep valleys. Up on the peaks and high passes it was bitterly cold, but down in the valleys it was hot and steamy. In some of the low places the tropical vegetation was often so dense that we could only move along the narrow trails, while flocks of screeching green parrots flew over our heads, and thousands of insects swarmed around us. To keep them off, Master smeared a smelly substance on our coats, but when he had used it all, we had to defend ourselves by swishing our tails, or by shaking our manes, kicking and stamping all the time.

Since I'm talking about manes and tails I must interrupt my story for a moment, for there are a few things I'd like you to know about them.

Off and on I've seen horses whose tails had been cut off so short that only little stumps were left. At first I thought these poor horses had been born with this deformity, but later I found out that stupid and cruel men cut off the unfortunate animals' tails. Often several of the tail-bones are chopped off, and, as you can imagine, this is a very painful operation. But not only that. Once the poor horse has no tail left he can't protect himself against flies.

I suppose most of you have noticed that we can twitch our skins to frighten away insects. If you have a good look at a horse you will see that he can't move the skin on the hind-quarters and hind-legs. That's why nature has given us tails, for with them we can protect ourselves, and when we run and turn we use them as rudders.

Next time you see a man riding or driving a horse whose tail has been cut off, you just pass him and look the other way, for even if he is dressed up in riding-breeches, boots and spurs, and frowns with conceit, you may be sure that he doesn't know much about us horses. To be a good horseman—or horsewoman—a person must not only be able to ride well, but be able to understand, and know how to look after a horse.

Now let's go back into the mountains where I interrupted my story.

We had crossed the whole of Bolivia, and were now in a country called Peru. I've already told you that it was very cold up on these high mountains, and that the trails were often very bad and dangerous. Here and there they were cut out of mountain walls, and were so narrow that if an animal had come in the opposite direction, the two couldn't have passed each other, and it would have been equally impossible for them to turn round. Luckily there are only a few of these death-traps, and when men come to them they dismount and go afoot to see if anybody is coming in the opposite direction.

It has happened that two careless travellers have unexpectedly met in one of those narrow places; and as they couldn't turn their mules, or make them walk backwards, the man who managed to pass was the one who shot first, killing the other and his mount, sending the two hurtling down the precipice. The further we went, the worse our trail became. Sometimes it lead us into cold regions, high up above the clouds, and then down into steaming tropical valleys. The man who had joined Master was beginning to feel very ill, for he wasn't used to the open air and the hardships of such a journey. His face was swollen, and his skin had cracked, and both his hands were sore and bleeding; but in spite of this he managed to keep up with us. Disregarding Master's warnings he scratched himself after gnats and mosquitoes had bitten him; and, as finger-nails are never perfectly clean, he contracted blood-poisoning which very nearly cost him his life.

One morning I was picking my way along a narrow trail. On my left was the solid wall of the mountain, and on my right a steep incline which ended abruptly at the edge of a frightfully deep precipice. From where we were, a big river below us looked like a winding thread of silver.

Suddenly a piece of rock under my right hind-leg gave way, and before I realised what was happening, I shot down the incline towards the gaping chasm. I had already closed my eyes in order not to see the giddy height down which I was about to fall to certain death, when I suddenly hit a tree which stopped my rapid slide. For a moment I thought the trunk would snap, but luckily it was strong enough to support my weight. From my perilous position I couldn't see the trail above, but I heard Master's voice and Mancha's snorts of fear. In despair I neighed until I saw Master who came clambering down the incline towards me.

Realising that I was more or less safe, as long as I didn't move from the little tree against which I was still leaning, I stood quite still and trembled, whilst I watched Master come nearer and nearer.

After what seemed an eternity, kindly Indians arrived on the scene, and at once helped to save me. To do this, ropes were tied around me. When all was ready Master gave a signal, whereupon the sturdy Indians above pulled as hard as they could, and thus assisted me to climb back to safety.

When I was once more on the narrow trail, Mancha sniffed me affectionately, while the sturdy natives stroked my trembling body. I was so glad to be alive that I forgot all about poor Master, who was still down below rescuing the saddle and other things he had taken off me.

At last, however, he appeared on the trail, perspiring so much that one might have thought he had just come out of a river. He slapped his big hat on the ground, and, seating himself on a rock, had a good laugh. After having rested for a while, he gave the good Indians some coins and cigarettes, whereupon they departed. I was very careful after that, and never trod on another loose piece of rock.

Sometimes we zig-zagged up or down steep trails for whole days, and if we happened to spend the night in one of the hot valleys we were attacked by blood-sucking animals, called "vampire bats." These repulsive creatures acted with such cunning that we never felt them bite us to suck our blood.

Sometimes, after having struggled over rough and dangerous trails for a whole day, we were so tired that we slept in spite of the thousands of insects which buzzed around us.

Vampires begin their attacks by circling round and round the horse or mule, and when he feels drowsy the bat slowly settles on him, all the time fanning the wings to make the victim feel cool. Whilst doing this the vampire bites through the hide with his tiny sharp teeth, doing this so gently that no pain is felt. Both Mancha and I were bitten by many of these horrid vampire bats, but when Master found a way to keep them off us we were never again troubled by them. He used to sprinkle strong Indian pepper on our backs, or rubbed us down with a strong-smelling disinfectant, which these repulsive pests disliked, and therefore made them keep away from us.

Up in those mountain regions of Peru only Indians live. They are peace-loving, and spend their time in looking after their crops in the small fields and plantations which are in the valleys and on terraces along some of the mountain-sides.

When we had crossed most of the mountains, we came to a railway where Master's sick companion left us, after he had got rid of his two mules. The poor man was very ill; and I'm sure he'll never again want to travel in those rough and wild mountains.

Instead of following the railway line—the first one we had seen for a long time—we returned to the mountains.

Heavy rains were pouring down on us every day, and the rivers were so swollen and turbulent that it was very dangerous to cross them by swimming. You should see and hear some of these wild mountain rivers, when they come romping down the deep valleys in full flood! Big rocks and stones bounce and roll down with the seething, hissing and foaming waters, shaking the very mountains and filling the air with a noise like thunder.

One day, as we were slowly picking our way along a mountain-side, we had a narrow escape from death. For several days rain had come down in torrents, and all the mountain trails were transformed into swift streams, making progress very slow and dangerous, for we often tripped over projecting points of rock or stones, which were invisible owing to the water which came rushing down the steep trails.

We were following one of these which led along a very steep slope, and I was just wondering when we would get our next meal when I heard a strange rumbling sound above us. The noise was so mysterious that Mancha and I stopped dead and began to tremble with fear. Within a few seconds the rumbling sound had grown to the most terrific thunder, and the ground on which we stood rocked and trembled so violently that we almost fell. Just then a sudden gust of wind hit me with terrific force, and before I knew what was happening, I was wrapped in a dense cloud of dust which almost choked me.

I don't know how long I stood there, for when I was able to see and think again I only heard a loud rumble, deep down below us. Master and Mancha were still standing near me, and, having looked at each other, we turned to see what on earth all this commotion could have been.

Only a few yards behind us the whole side of the mountain had been torn away, and the narrow trail, over which we had passed a few seconds before, had disappeared. I was so startled by this scene of devastation that it took me quite a while to realise that this had been a land-slide, and that it had only missed us by a few yards.

Some of the rivers were so swollen and turbulent, and many trails so bad and dangerous that we had to make several big détours to avoid running unnecessary risks. Once or twice we were hopelessly lost up in those mountains, and as we had only very little to eat, we had a pretty rotten time of it for a week or two.

In those parts the mountains look as if they had been split and cracked by gigantic thunderbolts, and some of the precipices and canyons are several thousand feet deep. More than once our trail led straight towards frightful chasms, across which the Indians had built frail hanging bridges. When I saw the first of these primitive constructions it made me feel quite ill and giddy; and when Master went to inspect it, and even walked to the other side, I thought he must have gone crazy. Just imagine my surprise when he came back, and, after having tied me to a stone, went over to Mancha and led him towards the bridge! My pal seemed to be as surprised as I was, for when he realised that Master wasn't joking, but really wanted him to cross the giddy and swinging bridge, he sniffed it and tested its strength by stamping on it with one foot. Master kept on telling Mancha that it was all right, and asked him to be a good boy, and just follow him quietly.

I felt cold ripples run down my back when I saw my two pals step on the bridge which sagged terribly in the middle, and swung to and fro like a hammock. I wondered if it was strong enough to bear the weight of the two, and I was afraid that the flooring of sticks and twigs would give way. Looking at the frightful drop down to the river below made me feel sick in my stomach. In despair I neighed; but Mancha was far too busy to answer; for now, step by step, he picked his way. I could have yelled with joy when my dear friends safely reached the other side, but at the same moment it suddenly dawned on me that it would be my turn next.

As soon as Mancha was on solid rock again, he looked across the chasm and called proudly:

"Did you watch me? Now let's see what you can do!"

I don't mind admitting that I was almost ill with fear, but when I heard this I shouted back:

"All right, old chap; keep your eyes well open, and you'll learn something!"

When Master had untied me he led the way towards the bridge. Trying to look brave I didn't even halt to sniff or test its strength, but I just followed Master, and soon reached the middle of the bridge. The beastly thing sagged so much with our weight that we were down in a deep hollow where we swayed from side to side till I thought we would fall down. I had made up my mind not to look into the depth below, but when the bridge swung so much that we had to stop, I got a glimpse of the river, deep down below us. For a moment I thought my knees were about to give way, and I felt as if some invisible being were trying to pull me over the edge. Luckily, just then Master spoke to me, and to give me courage, patted my neck. When he moved on again I followed without knowing what I was doing, for my head was "swimming," and I felt as if I were walking upside-down.

Once we had passed the sagging middle of the bridge we had to go uphill, which made progress much more easy. Realising that I was nearing safety, I hurried so much that my weight made the bridge bob up and down violently; and Master had to hold on for all he was worth to save himself from falling overboard.

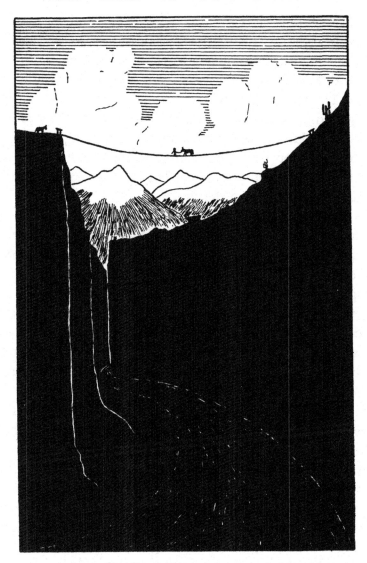

Mancha watches Gato cross a hanging bridge

At last, puffing and panting with fright and excitement, I reached Mancha, who sarcastically said:

"I thought you were going to teach me something, but it strikes me you didn't see the joke when you got to the middle of the bridge. The way you hurried off it makes me think that you're mighty glad to be over here, and on solid rock once more!"

The way Mancha teased me was most annoying, so I replied: "Oh, when I stopped I just wanted to look down to see what could have frightened you, and I only hurried to come and tell you how much I enjoyed the fun."

We were just going to start a fight when Master came and told us that we had been so good that he would travel no further that day. He then led us towards a hut near there, and after he had unsaddled he brought us as much fodder as the Indians were willing to sell.

As we were chewing and munching our well-earned reward we occasionally looked towards the beastly bridge, and every time we caught each other's eye we winked and giggled inwardly, for we both knew that we had been in a blue funk: a fact neither of us was willing to admit.

We both hoped that we would never come to another such bridge, but, as it happened, we had to cross several more before we were out of the vastness of the Peruvian Andes.

Once we were caught in a blizzard. It snowed so hard that we couldn't see more than a yard or two ahead of us, and the wind was so strong that we weren't able to travel without running the risk of having a serious fall. Finding a rock which broke the force of the wind, we huddled together behind it, and waited for several hours till the fury of the elements had abated.

One morning we reached a high peak where there was a lot of snow. From there—for two long days—we stumbled down a narrow and very rough trail which led towards the Pacific Ocean. Up in the mountains it had been very cool, and often even bitterly cold, but in the low-land near the coast it was very hot.

After a short journey through stifling heat and dust, we arrived at a picturesque old town called Lima, which was built by the Spaniards, and to-day is the capital of the Republic of Peru. You should have seen all the people who came to look at us when we trotted through the streets! One might have thought they had never before seen a horse.

We had a good vacation in Lima where everybody was very good to us. We were just beginning to feel at home in our stables, when Master again saddled us up and guided us towards the north. This time, however, he didn't take us back to the mountains, but made us go into the sandy deserts, which extended all along the coast of Peru.

I think Mancha can tell the next part of our story better, so I'll let him go on with it.

STORY SEVENTEEN

*In which Mancha takes you through burning deserts, quick-
sands and mud, and tells various interesting and amusing
stories*

SOMETIMES, when I'm in a dreamy mood, and in my mind's eye
wander back over our long trail, I wonder which was the most
difficult part we crossed. If anybody asked me this question, I
really couldn't answer it, for I simply can't decide which is
worst: high, cold and barren mountains; blizzards and deep
precipices; burning deserts and lack of water; tropical swamps
with fever and insects; dense jungles with perilous rivers and
reptiles, or civilised countries—with highways and thousands of
speeding cars. Honestly, I can't make up my mind which of
these I hated most, for they're all bad and, sometimes, dangerous.

.　　　.　　　.　　　.　　　.　　　.　　　.

We hadn't gone far from Lima when we came to vast sandy
deserts. As far as we could see there was nothing but golden-
yellow sand, which, in some places, was piled up so high by the
wind that it formed high hills which looked like huge waves
in a storm. As the wind changes from one quarter to another,
these sand-hills and dunes are being shifted about all the time.

Step by step we went nearer towards the equator which, as
you know, is an imaginary line that goes around the middle of
the world, half-way between the North and South Poles. You

also know that near both Poles it's very cold, and that, as you
go towards the equator, it gets hotter and hotter. If you remember this, and look at a map which shows the Peruvian deserts
I'm now talking about, you'll be able to imagine the heat we had
to endure there.

For whole days we waded through soft sand, which was often
so hot that it burnt through our hoofs. In those deserts we didn't
see a single blade of grass, and we only found water when we
came to the few rivers which flow down from the distant
mountains. Near these rivers, which are separated by vast
deserts, we came to miserable villages where drinking water is
often so scarce that it is sold in old petrol cans, which long-
suffering donkeys carry from house to house.

Sometimes it was so hot that we would have died if we had
tried to cross these deserts in the day-time, so Master rested us
near a river, and then travelled when the moon showed us the
way.

Often we went down on the flat sandy beach where the waves
of the Pacific Ocean broke. You talk about lovely beaches, but
you ought to see those along the coast of Peru. As far as you can
see there's nothing but golden sand and white foam of breaking
waves, which look lovely with the deep greenish-blue of the
ocean. You never see a human being, but instead, you have the
company of countless sea-birds, which are quite tame, because
nobody ever disturbs them.

At first the pelicans' huge beaks amused me, and so did the
crabs when they ran away sideways. Occasionally we saw seals,
who came to look at us; and once even some huge whales. The
three of us had a good look at a dead one that had been washed

H

up on the beach. Yes, we saw something new every day, even out in the desolation of deserts.

One day I watched a seagull who was stealing fish from pelicans, and I couldn't help laughing when I saw how this was done.

Every time a pelican caught a fish he threw it up into the air, whereupon the gull swooped down like an arrow. Before the fish reached the pelican's enormous beak, the cunning thief had snatched it away; and all the poor pelican got was a beakful of air.

The way I'm talking might make you think that travelling along the coast was all fun; but now I'll show you that it really wasn't as pleasant as you might think.

It's all very well talking about lovely beaches, golden sands and foaming surf, but they are of little use if no fresh water or food can be found near them.

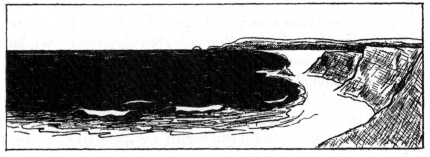

The desert coast of Peru

Supposing something had happened to one of us out there. What would we have done? There's no telling, but I guess the birds of the air would have had a feed; and to-day our bleached bones would be scattered on the shimmering sands to serve travellers as a warning to keep out of these desolate regions.

Just think; one of the deserts we had to cross was nearly 100 miles long! Although there wasn't a chance to find a drop of water till we reached a river on the far side, we managed to get there in twenty hours.

In that neighbourhood we had to swim across several very wide rivers, on the flat banks of which there was danger of being caught in quicksands. We had to be very careful, for if a horse or a man steps into one of these, he is slowly sucked down.

We had one or two narrow escapes, but thanks to our instincts we always avoided these death-traps, even if Master was not aware of their presence, and tried to guide us straight towards them.

Long before white men ever discovered this land, Indian tribes used to live in places which now are deserts. Although these tribes have long ago died out, the ruins of their villages and towns can still be seen. Near most of these ruins the ancient Indians used to bury their dead, but with the passing of years the sand has been shifted by the wind, and now bones and skulls can be seen lying all over these old burial grounds.

The natives tell many strange ghost stories about these old graves, for all over the world ignorant people are superstitious, and many are more afraid of the harmless dead than they are of the wicked people who may be in their midst.

Several times I listened to natives who told Master hair-raising stories about the dead dancing at night, and I also heard yarns about huge monsters which are supposed to live in caves along the coast.

When we came to ancient ruins and burial grounds, Master sometimes entered underground passages in which the Indian chiefs were buried; and more than once he brought out mummies which were fully dressed and well preserved. He also found pots and vases which, however, he could not take with him, because there was no room in the saddle-bags.

In a filthy little village along the coast, a man gave Master a little whip. I was quite surprised when I saw him accept the gift, for I wondered what on earth he intended to do with it.

I had forgotten all about this little whip, when, as we were about to start, Master came towards us, flicking it against his boot. I didn't mind this a bit, but when we were plodding through the soft sand, and he absent-mindedly kept on touching my flanks with the beastly thing, I began to get annoyed. Several times I tried to kick the whip out of his hand, but even this didn't seem to make him realise that I was getting really sick of all this flicking business.

At last I thought the time had come to put a stop to all this nonsense, so I gave Gato a sly wink.

Master was almost asleep, but with every stride I made, his right arm moved up and down like the handle of a pump, and every time it came down, his little whip tickled me in the ribs. Suddenly, with a snort, I put my head between my fore-legs, at the same time giving a good buck, which was sufficient to make Master loop-the-loop and land in the soft sand in front of me.

You should have seen his face! For a few moments he didn't seem to know what had happened, and he only realised where he was when I pushed my head close up to his and snorted into one of his ears. The three of us had a good laugh, and then we continued our journey as if nothing had happened; and when we came to the next miserable settlement, Master gave his little whip to a boy.

What with deserts, quicksands and wide rivers, I was glad when we again headed towards the mountains, for I knew that up in the high places it would be much cooler. Along the sandy coast of Peru it was often so hot that one could have fried eggs in the fierce rays of the sun. When we were lucky enough to find water, it was warm and had a nasty taste, and our fodder was so bad and insufficient that we had lost a lot of weight.

The next country we came to is called Ecuador, which is the Spanish word for "equator." The republic has been given this name because the equator passes through the middle of it.

Most people think that it must have been very hot when we crossed "the line," as sailors call the equator; but, as a matter of fact, it was very cool, and not far above us were regions of eternal snow.

If we had continued along the coast, and had crossed the equator in the lowland near the sea, it would have been frightfully hot. Up in the beautiful highland of Ecuador the climate is cool and bracing, and lovely flowers and strawberries grow there all the year round.

Mind you, it was no easy matter to reach the vast high valleys, for after we left the desert coast of Peru, we had to climb over many high mountains, or were obliged to fight our way along deep ravines, and sometimes through forests and dense jungles.

In low places the trails were often terrible, the mud and slime being so deep that it sometimes reached half-way up our flanks, covering us with a mass of thick and smelly mud which consisted chiefly of earth, clay and rotten leaves.

In this neighbourhood we met with new dangers, one of the greatest being deep mud-holes, which, like quicksands, are treacherous death-traps. Woe to the man or animal who steps into one of these harmless looking mud-holes! Unless somebody is near with a lasso or a rope, the victim is doomed to a horrible death, for the more it struggles and fights, the quicker it sinks into the black slime in which it finally disappears.

In spite of enduring hardships, we had many good laughs. Talking about the mud reminds me of a funny incident that happened to Master while we were wading along one of these awful mud-trails.

The smelly mire and water was getting so deep that he had to lift his feet to keep them dry, sitting on the saddle with his legs crossed like a Turk. Gato—who was carrying him—happened to stumble over a log, and poor Master rolled over backwards and tumbled into the slime, which was as thick as pea-soup!

When he came to the surface he coughed, spluttered and spat, and when he had recovered his breath he used such language that I looked up to the top of the trees and pretended to be listening to the screeching and chattering parrots and monkeys, who appeared to be as amused as I was.

In certain parts of Ecuador we saw some most interesting and picturesque Indians. One tribe is called "Runa," and another "Jivero." The Runa Indians are quite civilised, being good farmers and hard workers. The men have long hair, which often reaches down to their elbows.

The Jivero Indians are sometimes very wrongly called "Head-

Hunters." They are rather ugly, having flat noses, high cheek-bones, thick bulgy lips and slit eyes, like Chinamen. To adorn themselves they make deep cuts into their cheeks, noses and fore-heads. These cuts are filled with paints of different colours, and they never come off, as I've already told you in Story Fifteen. I thought the Jiveros looked very ugly with the coloured slashes on their faces, but obviously these Indians think other-wise. Somehow, I could never understand the taste of human beings, for I have seen many white people who wore clothes and hats which would make even "head-hunters" laugh, not to men-tion the paint and powder with which many civilised women plaster their faces.

I nearly forgot that I was going to tell you why the Jivero Indians are sometimes called head-hunters.

As a matter of fact, Indians fight much less than white men do, and even when they are at war, only very few men meet their death. If a Jivero kills an enemy he cuts off his head and puts it through a process of shrinking, until it's only about the size of a big fist. Somehow the features don't change, and the face remains recognisable.

Every day the victorious Jivero talks to the little head of his dead enemy, saying how sorry he is that he had to kill him. To ensure that the defunct warrior's spirit can speak no ill of the victor, the lips of the shrunken head are stitched together with wool.

The Jiveros do most of their fighting and hunting with bows and arrows, or with spears, and they are also very skilful with the blow-guns you already know about.

For special festive occasions they dress up in their gala attire, the dresses being as strange as they are colourful. The men wear head-dresses made of stuffed birds and lovely feathers, and round their necks, arms and legs, they coil long beads which are made of seeds and teeth of animals. For further adornment Jivero Indians wear bracelets and collars consisting of many brightly-coloured wings of insects, which sparkle like gems; and sometimes the men's dark bodies are covered with aprons made of hundreds of marvellously coloured breasts of humming-birds. Round their ankles and calves the dancers suspend shells of certain snails. These shells make noises like the tinkling of many small bells.

Where the Jiveros live it is very hot, but in spite of being used to a tropical climate, they can endure the icy chills of the high mountains. They sometimes cross the mountains and visit white men to exchange medicinal herbs, rare pets, beads, and gold nuggets for whatever they wish to obtain in return. Usually they want to take home knives, gunpowder and rifles, for during recent years, even the primitive Jiveros have found out that white men's firearms are very deadly and can kill at long range, when properly used.

Adventure is often found when and where one least expects it. This proved to be true when we arrived at a small settlement in the interior of Ecuador.

Master had thrown the pack and saddles on the mud-floor in a miserable and dirty little hut. When he had paid natives to go and cut grass for us, he groomed our coats and examined our hoofs to see if they had been damaged by the stony trail we had travelled on all day.

Presently the natives returned with bundles of grass, and an

Indian woman brought Master a wooden bowl which was filled with steaming beans.

Whilst he was squatting near us enjoying his food, a half-naked Indian boy looked on with longing eyes. When Master had satisfied his appetite he offered the boy what was left over; and you should have seen how that youngster devoured the food! Goodness; I thought he was going to swallow the bowl as well!

Since the Indians brought us plenty of good grass, and Master could also eat nutritious food, he decided to stay in this settlement for two or three days, and thus give us a chance to regain strength for the next stage of the journey.

Every day, and all day long, that Indian boy of the beans was near the hut where we stayed. When Master took us to a stream to give us a drink and a good wash, the boy followed and gave a helping hand, and in return for his services Master gave him big bowls full of beans and coffee.

Gato and I got to like this youngster who told Master that he was an orphan. The poor kid was dirty and very thin, but I wasn't surprised at that, for everybody in the place treated him like a stray dog; and he probably hadn't had a decent meal for weeks, until we arrived.

The boy had long hair in which his only friends lived, and his body was covered with a dirty and torn cape. As he had never worn boots, his feet were as tough as leather, and his toes were apart, like the fingers of a half-open hand.

The day before we left, I heard the kid ask Master to take him with us. He said he could walk and trot to keep up with us afoot, that he knew how to build fires quickly, and that he could do many things which are very useful when men travel in the wilds.

Master seemed to think matters over for a while, and then he suddenly got up, took some scissors and cut off the boy's long hair. Having done this, he gave him some disinfectant and soap and told him to go and wash himself in the stream.

Accordingly, the boy left, and when he returned he looked so clean that I hardly recognised him. Master then went to a hut where he bought him a sort of jacket, a pair of trousers and a warm woollen cape.

Gato and I were so surprised at all this that we stopped eating. We watched with bulging eyes, wondering what was going to happen next.

The boy couldn't speak Spanish very well, and was obviously used to talking in some Indian tongue which neither Master nor we understood. However, we got on pretty well, and in the evening when we were again led to the stream for a drink, I heard Master tell the youngster that the trail ahead of us would be very long and often difficult, and that he would have to help him to look after the pack and saddles which—more than once—had been tampered with by thieves when he had taken us to water or had gone in search of fodder.

He told the boy that we would leave the settlement before daybreak, and that he wanted to see the sunrise from a distant ridge towards which he pointed.

Both Gato and I sniffed the boy, for now we knew that he had joined our expedition. Victor, as Master had named the boy, soon got to love us as much as we loved him, and even when we played tricks on each other, we only did it to cheer us up when we felt dull and wanted to have a little fun.

In the republic of Ecuador there are practically no roads, and therefore trails are the only means of communication with the interior. Where such trails connect villages and small towns, so many mules and horses travel over the same path, that regular steps have been made where countless hoofs have trodden for many years. Where the ground is soft, the hollows between these steps are often so deep that an animal with short legs touches the ground with his belly. Since all these steps are the same distance apart, we had to learn to take very short and even strides, but until we could do this we often stumbled, and even had some nasty falls.

Victor soon proved to be a good traveller, and made himself useful in many ways. You should have seen the way he climbed up the steep mountains, and how he skipped from rock to rock, joking and laughing all the time.

When camp was pitched for the night, it took him only a few moments to find three big stones, place them together in the shape of a triangle to support the cooking-pot, and then light the fire. Whilst the burning wood crackled and the smoke curled up through the trees, he looked for a nice dry spot, where he spread the blankets and fixed up a mosquito-net, having the shape of a small tent.

In the meantime Master groomed us, or went off to shoot some birds, which were usually stewed with rice and beans.

If it happened to be raining, camping in the wilds wasn't so nice. Master hadn't a tent with him, for even a small one would have been an extra weight and bulk for us to carry. When the weather was bad he just used a big, square sheet of waterproof cloth which had a slit in the middle. By sticking his head through this slit he could use this cloth as a cloak, and if he wanted to sleep under it, he staked it down and propped it up in such a manner as to make it into a tiny tent which had the shape of an upside-down V.

When Master was quite sure that Victor was game to go with us wherever we went, he promised to buy him a pony and saddle.

I can't tell you how proud and delighted the boy was when we left the next village we had come to, for he was seated on a lovely black Indian pony which had a long thick mane and flowing tail. Our new four-footed friend was so small that Master named him "Chico," which is the Spanish word for *tiny*.

We soon made friends with the new member of our little expedition, and all went well till he tried to boss me.

Master and Victor had cut down some bamboo creepers which they heaped up for us to nibble off the leaves. Although this is rotten fodder it's the only kind we often had. Sometimes Master cut the soft centre shoots out of palm trees and chopped them up with a large bush-knife.

Now; that evening, when the bamboo creepers had been cut down and heaped up before us, Chico wanted to have all to himself. Before I knew what was happening, the greedy little fellow started to bite and kick so fast, and in all directions, that I first of all thought a whole herd of horses was fighting us. When I recovered from my first surprise, I laid back my ears and gave a snort of warning. This, however, didn't seem to make the slightest difference to the little black fellow who went on kicking furiously till he got me in the ribs.

This made me so mad that I forgot all the good manners I had learnt, and so, with a squeal of anger and pain, I flew at Chico and went for him until Master interfered.

That night the greedy little fellow was tied to a thick creeper, where he had time to think over which of us was boss. Whenever I looked at him he trembled all over, for he thought I was going to give him another beating.

Like a good-natured fool, Gato never protested; and the result was that from that day on the pony always bossed him, though he took mighty good care to leave *me* alone.

Still, in spite of these little squabbles, we were soon the best of friends, and never again had a serious fight.

By degrees we came to parts where white men lived, and where the trails were better. We passed quite near some beautiful snow-covered mountains, which made it hard to believe that we were practically on the equator. I shall never forget a lovely cone-shaped volcano called Cotopaxi. Like a glittering sugar-loaf it rises high up into the deep blue sky, its pointed crater every now and again puffing out a cloud of vapour.

There are several other volcanoes in Ecuador. Some emit black smoke, fire and lava, and sometimes break out in eruptions which destroy every plant and tree for miles around, even causing the death of men and animals who cannot flee in time.

We were very thankful when we reached Quito, the capital of Ecuador. This lovely old Spanish town is situated high up in the mountains, and is practically on the equator.

The trails had been very trying, and we had eaten so little, and such bad fodder, we were in sore need of food and a good rest.

Master found a nice field on the outskirts of the town, where he turned us loose. Whilst we rested there and nibbled as much of the juicy grass as we could hold, he came twice every day to give us a nose-bag full of oats and corn, the taste of which we had almost forgotten.

I can't tell you how delicious the grass seemed, for in many places we had to live on any kind of weed or leaves. Very often Master had to watch us carefully, to make sure that we didn't eat poisonous plants which were unknown to us, because they don't grow where we were born and raised.

After a delightful rest near the old town of Quito, we continued our journey north.

The country was beautiful, and the climate so bracing and cool that it didn't seem true that we were crossing the equator. In those regions the sun is straight overhead at midday, and therefore, if you planted a pole in the ground, and took good care to make it stand perfectly straight, it would throw no shadow at noon.

Before we crossed the "line" we were on the southern half of the world, but as soon as we were across this invisible division of our planet, we stepped into the northern half, or *hemisphere*, as it's called.

We had only travelled two or three days from Quito when we again came to rough mountainous country; here we had to descend into frightfully hot valleys, only to climb up steep slopes again until we were high up above the clouds where it was bitterly cold.

The next, and last country we came to in South America, is called Colombia. But I'll now let Gato go on with the story.

STORY EIGHTEEN

*In which Gato says what he thinks of insects and snakes,
and tells a sad story about the death of an unknown hero,
and gives an amusing account of how a clever dog fooled
crocodiles*

BEFORE I had traversed certain regions in South America, I never
would have believed that such scorching heat and bitter cold can
be encountered during a day's march.

In some of the valleys it was so hot that the air near the ground
rose in shimmering waves, and the rays of the sun were so fierce
that it felt as if they were burning through the hair, skin and
flesh, penetrating to our very bones. As I staggered along I was
often half dazed, and thought I was walking between two fires:
one above my head, and the other under my hoofs. To make
things even worse, swarms of gnats and sand-flies attacked me,
making me feel as if hundreds of tiny pins were being stuck into
me. Often some of these agonising insects got into our eyes and
noses. There's no need for me to tell you how unpleasant this
was, for surely you've had a gnat or a particle of sand in an eye,
and therefore you know how very painful this can be.

As soon as we had crossed these valleys, which felt like hot
burning furnaces, we had to climb up steep mountains, where
even the best trails were frightful.

The higher we went, the cooler did the air become, and when
we finally reached the wind-swept tops of these high mountains

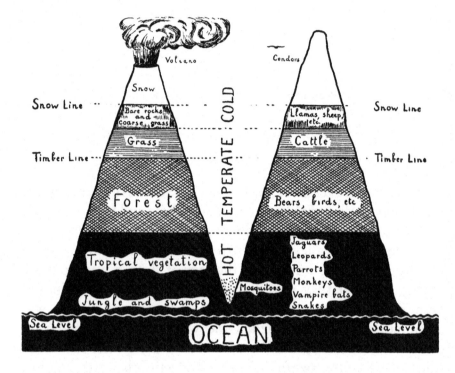

we felt so cold that we shivered till we thought our teeth would fall out of our mouths.

The marvellous views we sometimes had from these peaks made up for the discomforts we had to endure.

Far below us, the tropical mists looked like a vast angry sea, out of which the mountain tops stuck, like fairy islands with glittering peaks of white.

Master always avoided spending the night in these high places, where there was no grass for us, and no fuel for a fire to protect us against the biting frosts.

He usually tried to pitch camp half-way down the mountains, where the atmosphere was mild, but, unfortunately, this wasn't always possible, for we needed water and grass, and they were often only to be found in the valleys. Master always tried new tricks to protect us against insects and vampire bats. One day he had a brain-wave, and tried a new experiment on us. Whenever I remember this I laugh until my stomach aches and tears roll out of my eyes. This is how it happened.

We were in a very hot region where insects tormented us till we nearly went mad. Sometimes, to get rid of the blood-suckers, we dashed into thick bushes, where we moved our bodies forwards and backwards to brush off the stinging, itching and buzzing pests. As soon as we came out of our simple but efficient scratching machines, we were again covered with thousands of these hungry and ferocious blood-suckers. Since we couldn't stay in bushes for ever, we had to come out sooner or later, and just let the insects feed on us.

Master had been out shooting, and when he returned to the camp he brought with him a bunch of big feathers. With the assistance of Victor he tied these together with bits of sticky tape and string, making three things which looked like bunches of flowers.

His idea was to tie these bunches of feathers to the ends of our tails, and thus enable us to swish off flies where our tails couldn't reach.

His plan would have been a good one, if only he had told us about it before he tied these bright feathers to the ends of our tails. As it happened, he and Victor got busy fixing on these contraptions, and as we were eating we never turned round to see what was being done to us.

I don't remember which one of us was first to swish his tail, but the fact is that the three of us got a fright together. When we saw these coloured things behind us, we bolted for dear life, only to find that, no matter where or how fast we raced, they followed us wherever we fled to get away from them. We scattered in all directions, through trees and bushes, paying no attention to Master and the boy, who called to us in voices of despair.

When I realised that by running I couldn't get rid of the terrifying thing behind me, I started to buck and kick and spin round and round—like a puppy with a wasp on its tail. When I was so tired that I could hardly move, I finally stopped. Suddenly I heard some wild trampling in the bushes near me; and presently Chico came dashing through a clearing, running like a black cat with a dog after it, the dog in this case being the bunch of feathers at the end of his tail.

I believed that my bunch of feathers had left me and was now chasing after Chico. This comforting thought made me sigh with relief, and as I did so I swished my tail to fight off the insects which had again gathered round me.

What a fright I had just then, for, suddenly, when I least expected it, that mysterious bunch of feathers reappeared again, hitting me square in the chest!

Although I was tired and out of breath, I bolted as if a thousand pumas were after me. I fled through open spaces and dense jungle, and when I rounded a thick cluster of bushes I saw Mancha who was busy dancing a Patagonian war-dance. To my

amazement and consternation I saw that he was being chased by that mysterious bunch of feathers which, I thought, had come after me when it couldn't catch Chico.

You see, at the time I didn't know that there were three bunches of feathers, and that Master had fixed one to Mancha's, Chico's and my tail.

This crazy sort of racing about went on till Master managed to lasso me. He hurriedly cut the feathers off my tail and threw a saddle on me, whereupon the two of us went to look for Mancha and Chico who were still missing.

After a long search through the jungle, we found our missing friends who were soon lassoed. It was getting dark when we returned to the camp where the three of us discussed our exciting adventure with the mysterious bunches of feathers. Every time a log in the camp-fire crackled or hissed we gave nervous jumps, for we thought the terror of the previous day had suddenly returned.

Master and Victor were so tired, and slept so soundly that they didn't even stir when the birds began their morning concert, parrots, cockatoos, wild turkeys and hundreds of other birds straining their lungs to make themselves heard above the others, all refusing to play second-fiddle in this musical free-for-all of the jungle.

I remember one occasion when Master made us return to a settlement we had left a few hours before. We were climbing up a mountain towards a very high pass, when the clouds became so threatening, and the wind so wild and cold, that it would have been dangerous to go on.

We, therefore, returned to the place where we had spent the previous night. There, at any rate, we would have comfort and something to eat, for the small settlement was tucked away in a tropical valley.

Up on the mountains a terrific storm raged for two days, and we were glad to be able to stay where we were, thankful to have escaped the fury of the elements.

When the weather cleared, and the mountain again became visible, we were filled with apprehension on seeing that it was covered with a mass of glittering white snow. The beauty of this sight was lost on us, for we realised how hazardous it would be to cross the heights until the snow had melted.

On the second evening of our forced stay in the settlement, a laden mule came staggering towards one of the huts; and when the natives saw the exhausted animal they got very excited and did a lot of talking and jabbering.

The heavy pack was quickly taken off the poor mule which was so weak that it even refused to eat the fodder kindly people had placed before it.

The natives recognised the animal as one of two which helped to carry the mail. We heard somebody tell Master that every two or three weeks a man had to cross the mountain to deliver letters and parcels which two hardy mules carried for him.

What could have happened to the man? Where was he, and the other mule? These questions were on everybody's lips.

Men, women and children cast fearful and apprehensive glances towards the towering mountain where the glittering snows seemed to give the answer which no one dared to put into words.

Dusk had already descended on the valley, and as the shadows of night crept higher and higher up the mountain, the white peak was transformed into a colossal glowing ember which seemed to melt until, finally, the last red point vanished into darkness.

First faintly, then clearer and clearer, twinkling stars penetrated through the black sky, which appeared to be no higher than the straw huts in which the fires and grease candles flickered, throwing grotesque shadows, adding mystery to these scenes of anxious suspense and mournful apprehension.

The tiny bright flashes of fire-flies floated through the air, blending to perfection with the twinkling stars which, together with the croaking and metallic "cluck-cluck" of hundreds of frogs, made me feel as if I were dreaming.

Gradually I became drowsy, and only mechanically continued to swish my tail, in vain efforts to keep off the mosquitoes
who never seem to rest. Presently everything became a blank;
and when I woke up, the stars were just beginning to fade.
Dawn was about to break.

Two days passed; but still the mail-carrier and the other mule
had not appeared. The snows up on the mountain had melted
considerably, and, therefore, a few men decided to accompany
Master and us to see if the missing man and mule could be found.

Frugal provisions were put into our pack, and, when several
mules had been saddled, our expedition set out, the inhabitants
of the settlement giving us a silent farewell.

After hours of stumbling and slipping over rocks and stones,
we arrived at the top of the mountain where we picked our way
along a high ridge, which was still covered with snow.

Whenever we stopped for a while, small clouds of vapour rose
from our hot and perspiring bodies, but the icy air of the heights
immediately dissolved these little clouds of steam into nothing.

After a long search, a man gave a signal and when we hurried
to the place where he had dismounted, we saw the figure of a
man who was lying behind a rock. He was covered with a
blanket, and looked as if he were asleep; and near him, tied to a
big stone, lay a mule which was still fully saddled. A member
of our party untied the straps, and when the mail-bags had been
placed on one of the men's animals, the stiff body of the dead
mail-carrier was tied into a saddle where it sat as if alive.

Master then took leave of the men who had been so kind to us;
and as we watched the little caravan of mourners retrace their
steps towards their humble homes, we could see the dead mail-

carrier who, even in death, seemed to defy the merciless mountain gods. With every stride of the mule, the stiff body was jolted from side to side, as it rode, step by step, towards the peaceful valley.

We continued on our way towards the unknown, glad that we had turned back before the storm broke out, for the natives of these regions say that the mountain gods have no mercy on human beings who invade their domain when they hold their secret council, which they always do behind a curtain of snow, when the icy winds howl over the peaks.

As on many former occasions, we were lucky to cross the mountain without mishap.

On the down-grade we often had a lot of fun, for if the trail was wet and slippery we sometimes had to slide for long distances. To do this we tucked our hind-legs under our bodies, and, spreading out our fore-legs, slid down the slopes like bears.

During one of these slides Master and I missed disaster by a few inches. It still makes me feel funny inside when I remember this narrow escape from death.

Heavy rains had fallen for several days. We had crossed a high mountain-pass, and were descending down towards the timber line, as the place is called where trees begin to grow. The narrow trail we followed soon became so slippery that we had to slide down-hill for long stretches. We were getting so good at this trick that we never fussed; and sometimes Master didn't even bother to dismount, but remained on us to enjoy the slide.

That day he and I went first, then came Mancha who was followed by Victor, mounted on Chico. Nothing exciting happened until I came to a place where the trail was so steep and soapy that I made ready for a good slide. Master gave a shout of joy as we shot down the hollow trail, but when we rounded a corner his merry calls to Victor changed into yells of alarm and warning, for, to our horror, we saw that the trail led straight past a deep precipice.

Realising the peril we were in, I struggled for dear life to stop sliding, but in spite of my frantic efforts, I shot ahead as if I were on ice. The next thing I remember is seeing a deep abyss shoot towards me; and when I thought my end had come, I heard a splashing and hissing noise, whereupon my body suddenly became cold. Immediately after, something hit me with a crash, which was followed by wild confusion.

Finding that I still had solid ground under my feet, I then looked about me, and to my surprise saw that Master, Victor, Mancha, Chico and I, were all in a heap.

My slide towards certain death had come to an end in a hole which was filled with water, and my friends—who had come behind—had crashed into me. Luckily we all came out of this wild mix-up with only a few knocks and bruises, and, of course, a nasty fright.

To make sure that none of us would slip, Master and Victor took their big bush-knives and hacked away until the trail was wide and safe enough to lead us past the edge of the precipice.

After this narrow escape, whenever we came to a place where we had to slide, Master or Victor always went down the trail afoot; and we were only made to slide down if the place was quite safe, but if there was danger of an accident, steps were hacked into the ground. You can imagine how long it took to make these; but, after all, "better late than never," as the old saying goes.

Entering the northern parts of Colombia, the country became flatter and flatter until we came to some vast swamps and dense jungles through which Master intended to take us to Panama. However, travelling became so difficult, and the country was so boggy and unhealthy that we were obliged to change our course, and head for a big river which is called Magdalene River.

These regions are very wild and swampy, and vast stretches are covered with dense jungles in which live jaguars, tiger-cats, and many snakes—big and small.

Ever since I saw my first snake I've been afraid of these reptiles, for instinct warned me that they can be very dangerous, some being so poisonous that they can even kill a horse.

As you know, some snakes are not poisonous, for many kinds are quite harmless, and even useful. If left undisturbed, the most deadly snakes don't attack horses or men, but if they get a fright they strike at the intruder of their domain.

People often tell terrible tales about the huge *anacondas,* as the biggest South American snakes are called, but most of these stories are not true, for in spite of the fact that some anacondas are over thirty feet in length, they are non-poisonous and afraid of men. Like most big snakes, they are *constrictors*—that is to say, they coil themselves around a victim and crush or strangle it.

If you look carefully at any snake, you can usually tell by looks if it is poisonous or not. The heads of venomous snakes are very flat and triangular, but the non-poisonous snakes' heads are rounder and have a "brain."

In some parts of South America there are huge black snakes

which are called *water-snakes*. They usually live near pools or rivers, where they hunt water-rats or similar animals.

The natives like water-snakes to live in their neighbourhood, for these reptiles do away with many animals which harm crops. Sometimes men catch a young one and keep it as a pet, for when it grows up it eats all the rats and mice which otherwise invade the huts.

It has happened that a grown-up water-snake mistook a baby for a big and tender rat; so, to make sure that the writhing black pet doesn't make the same mistake again, babies are put into baskets which hang suspended from a beam of the roof.

We were staying at a small ranch when, for the first time, I saw one of these water-snakes. A boy—who was riding a pony —came galloping towards the hut, dragging behind him a long black snake which was tied to the end of his lasso.

When his father saw what the boy had brought, he bent the youngster across his knee and spanked him till he squealed like a stuck pig.

Naturally, I thought the man must be angry with his son because he had toyed with danger; but I was wrong, for when he had finished spanking the boy I heard him tell Master that the beating was to be a lesson to the youngster never again to kill another of these useful water-snakes.

Most of the muddy and slow-flowing rivers in the North of Colombia are full of crocodiles and alligators which can be very dangerous. We had to be extremely careful how and where we swam across streams, for the ugly and repulsive brutes who lurk in many of these waters have been known to kill animals as big as myself.

For some strange reason crocodiles are particularly fond of eating dogs, who seem to be well aware of this. If a dog is foolish enough to swim in a stream where crocodiles are lurking he will be snatched up and dragged under before he has swum far.

Once I watched a rider cross a stream on his mount which was an excellent swimmer. A funny-looking mongrel had followed the man, but on reaching the bank of the stream the little tail-wagger acted as if he were water-shy. Instead of swimming across, he ran about fifty yards down-stream where he barked and barked as loudly as he could. Having kept this up for some time, he suddenly ran back as fast as he could, and with a wild leap plunged in where his master had crossed the stream. When he came to the surface he paddled for all he was worth, and soon reached the opposite bank where he romped about, yelping and barking with joy, every now and again shaking his dripping fur and rolling in the sand.

I wonder if you can guess why this little dog had run down the bank, and why he had barked there for so long before he raced back to plunge into the stream where his master had swum across?

The cunning little mongrel knew very well that crocodiles hear noises, even though they are under water; and that's why he had run down-stream to bark till all the crocodiles had assembled there. Although the reptiles were at the bottom, and could therefore not be seen, the dog knew when his chance had come, and then ran back to swim across where his master was waiting for him.

Victor had often been warned, and even scolded, for drinking water out of pools and ditches; and I often wondered why Master wouldn't let him drink whenever he was thirsty.

When we reached the Magdalene River we were put on a flat barge which was tied to the side of a very primitive boat. It was frightfully hot and stuffy, and, to make things worse, clouds of flies and mosquitoes tormented us day and night.

After two days on this awful boat, we came to a port called Cartagena—where we saw the Caribbean Sea—which is part of the Atlantic Ocean.

For two days we were kept in a filthy yard, and then Master led us down to the sea-beach where a big ocean liner was lying at anchor. After a long struggle we were finally hoisted on board; and when the sun set, our ship was so far from the shore that a black streak on the horizon was the last we saw of South America; and soon even this seemed to melt into one with the sea.

STORY NINETEEN

Mancha loses his temper. A sad parting. Life and adventure in the jungle. How jaguars are hunted

VICTOR had been ill for some time, and now he was so weak that he could hardly walk. I heard Master say that this was because the boy had been drinking bad water.

Before we had been put on board, Master had bought a bale of hay for us, and also some corn and oats. Although we had plenty to eat, we were glad when we saw the green shore come nearer and nearer, for we guessed that we would soon be taken off the beastly rolling ship.

I always listened when people talked near me, and that's how I found out that we were nearing a place called Panama.

As soon as our ship was safely tied to the quay, the passengers started going down the gangway. Master was having a long argument with the captain and some of the officers, and I heard him say that we could easily be led down the way the people went, but the officers simply wouldn't believe it, maintaining that horses weren't tight-rope-walkers, and that Master was talking nonsense.

I wish these men could have seen us go over some of the rope-bridges up in the Andes. If I hadn't been tied I would have given them a good nip in the pants for talking the way they did.

After a lot of arguing and fussing, one of the men brought a kind of a belt which was nearly two feet wide. Master looked at it for a while, and then put it round my body—like the girth of a saddle. I was so used to girths that I took next to no notice of what was being done to me, but when I suddenly felt that I was being hoisted into the air I got an awful fright.

At each end of the belt there was a strong loop through which a big iron hook had been passed; and this hook was fixed to a long steel cable, being part of a big crane which now lifted me high up into the air.

I've had a few good frights in my lifetime, but none ever made me feel worse than this one.

Up and up I went, and then, suddenly, I was swung over the ship's side. When I looked down I thought I was somewhere near the clouds, with the dock miles below me. I could see tiny men look up at me, and I thought I heard voices and even laughter. After a few awful moments I started going down, which made me feel as if I had left my stomach up in the air. The ground and people seemed to shoot towards me, and as I dropped lower and lower I was sure that the crowd of onlookers was amused and that many men laughed at me.

As soon as my feet touched solid ground I got so angry that I bucked, squealed and kicked until the belt, hook and cable fell off me. Feeling that I was free, I then let go my temper, and showed these people what we can do in Patagonia when we are really annoyed. I kicked over travelling-trunks and boxes, and made people run for dear life.

In the midst of all this excitement and panic I suddenly saw Master. This made me forget everything else, so I quickly trotted towards him, for I knew that he would sympathise with me, and that he would take me back to my companions, whom

I had not seen since I had been hoisted off the deck.

I was led to a corner and tied to a railing, where Gato and Chico joined me a little later. Both were so excited and nervous that they couldn't speak, but when we had calmed down a little we had a long conversation about our latest experience with Man.

Gato and Chico told me that they had also been hoisted off the ship by this mysterious steel crane, and they admitted that they had been so scared that they couldn't even show their disapproval, as I had done. Anyway, I'm glad that I got some of my own back, for I hate it when strangers take liberties with me, and think that I'm just any kind of fool to be toyed with and laughed at.

We had a lovely time in Panama, where everybody was very kind to us. We were put into a nice stable, where men in uniforms gave us good things to eat. These men spoke a language I had never heard before, but I soon found out that it's something like English, and that these men were American soldiers.

It was lovely in the clean stable, where we had soft beds of straw, and clear cool water whenever we wanted a drink. Every day people came to see us, some bringing us carrots and apples —tit-bits we had never tasted before.

Master sometimes took us out for a little exercise which did us a lot of good, for it's all very well eating a lot of good food and having a delightful rest, but to keep fit, even horses must use their lungs and muscles.

Several times we went to the Panama Canal to watch huge ships being put through the locks where they are raised over eighty feet above the level of the Atlantic Ocean. When this has been done they steam through a long lake, until, on the far side, they come to other locks where they are lowered to the level of the Pacific Ocean.

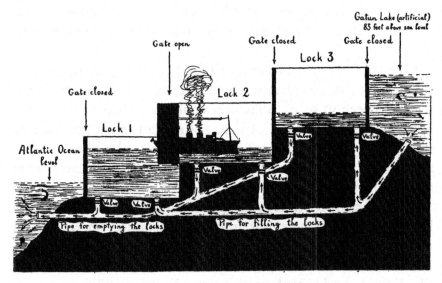

How the locks of the Panama Canal work

Before the Panama Canal was made, ships had to go all the way down to the far end of South America if they wanted to reach the Pacific Ocean.

If you look at a map you'll see how far this is, and you'll see that we were now very far from home, for we were born near the Magellan Straits through which the ships used to sail before the Panama Canal was built.

We hadn't seen Victor for some time, and we were wondering what could have happened to him. One day Master told us that the poor boy was very ill and that he was in a hospital. He

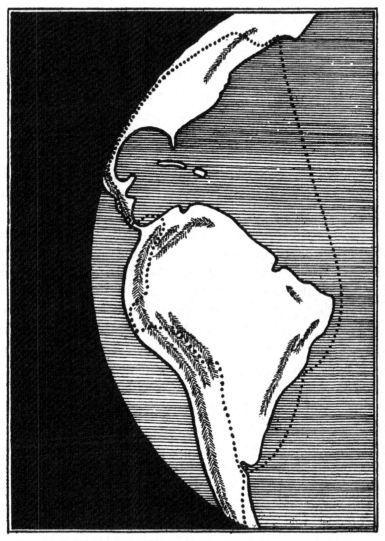

Thousands of miles—nearly half-way round the globe—
Mancha and Gato carried their master and pack; and then
returned home by sea

said that if Victor had done as he was told, and hadn't sneaked away from the camp to drink water, he wouldn't have been ill.

Some days later, when Master was making preparations to start out again, Victor appeared. We were so pleased to see him again that we nickered into his ears whilst he patted our necks. The boy stayed with us all day, and when evening came he asked Master if he might sleep on the straw in our stalls.

It was nice to have our little friend near us once more, and to eat hay out of his hands. Until late that night he fed and fondled us, and when he was getting sleepy he heaped up some straw and lay down on it.

Shortly after daybreak Master appeared, and with Victor's assistance led us to the place where the old saddles were kept. I knew at once that our delightful holidays had come to an end, and I guessed that more hardships were ahead of us.

The saddle-bags looked very full—a sure sign that we were going into wild places where all their contents would be needed.

Saddles and packs were strapped on us with great care, and when the shot-gun and the rifle had been fixed on top of the pack, we knew that we were ready to set out.

I couldn't understand why Chico was left in the stable, and it made me feel very sad to see Victor cry. During the night I had several times heard the boy sob; and thinking that he was still feeling ill, I softly nickered to him, for this is all a horse can do when one of his human friends is in distress.

A number of Master's friends had come to see us depart, and when I heard a man say that he would take good care of Victor, and promised that Chico's new home would be a good one, I began to understand.

Both Gato and I became very sad when we realised that we would soon have to part with Victor and Chico. In a way we were glad, for the boy was too weak to face another arduous journey through hot jungles; and Chico, though a good mountain pony, was not tough enough to survive weeks of tramping and struggling through tropical forests.

When Master started to say good-bye to all his friends and onlookers who had collected around us, Victor broke down completely. He clung to my neck and sobbed till I thought his heart would break, and then threw himself on the ground and hit the sand with his clenched fists.

I was almost glad when Master quickly mounted and made us trot away. When we passed our stable I heard Chico call to us. In answer we neighed: "Good-bye, Chico! You're lucky to stay where you are! We're going towards the unknown. Hope to see you again, some day!"

Before we rounded a corner we turned to have a last look at Victor. The kindly gentleman who had promised to look after him now stood with one hand on the boy's shoulder. A chorus of voices shouted: "Good-bye and good luck!" But above all these voices we heard one we had grown to love. This time it didn't sound as clear and merry as it had done up in the mountains when its owner skipped and jumped from rock to rock. Like a lost colt neighing, we heard our friend Victor call: "A Dios, Mancha y Gato!"

And then we hurried away as if ugly vampire bats were chasing us, for even we horses hate to leave good friends.

During our long journey we seldom had the luck to rest where we were really happy and comfortable. The places we liked best were those where there was plenty to eat, where the water was good, and the climate cool.

Unfortunately, it wasn't often that we found all these things, so we just had to put up with what there was, and make the best of it.

Panama was one of the few spots where we had a grand time, and therefore we were very sorry when we had to leave.

For the first two or three days we didn't feel a bit like going on, and we missed our friends, Victor and Chico. However, after having been on the march for a few days, we again settled down to hard work and discomforts; and Panama, the stables and the two friends we had left behind, seemed like memories of a dream. Occasionally a smell or noise brought back recollections of Patagonia, but the happy days of our youth seemed unreal, and I thought they were part of a story I had once heard, and which now flashed through my mind in a most mysterious manner. I shook my head and snorted, for what was the use of dreaming about the Past when we were face to face with a difficult Present?

The isthmus of Panama is only a little over forty miles across, but as we forged ahead it became wider and wider. For the first few days, travelling was easy, and if it hadn't been so hot we could have made much longer journeys.

In some places we came to open grassland, where we would have enjoyed ourselves but for hundreds of ticks and insects which attacked us.

Ticks live in the grass and on leaves. If a horse or a man

walks through the grass, masses of these tiny pests crawl up him, and then dig themselves into his flesh to suck blood. Once they have—what you might almost call—"taken root," they suck blood till they are puffed up and quite round. When a tick has been on his victim for a few days he looks like a small grey marble, and is so full of blood that he almost bursts.

You can imagine how we felt when hundreds of these ticks crawled over us. To make things even more maddening, it was so hot and stuffy that we were dripping with perspiration which ran into the sores on our skins, causing irritations which burnt like nettles.

Every day Master washed us and himself down with a disinfectant which he mixed with water. If he hadn't done this, I really believe we would have died.

Since the narrow strip of continent twists towards the West, we had to travel in that direction.

Gradually the grassland changed into forests, and as we forged ahead these became denser and denser.

At long intervals we came to some huts where we usually spent the night. These jungle abodes are as primitive as the people who live in them, for they merely consist of a steep roof which is made of dry palm-leaves, the open space below it being the kitchen and living-room. Between this ground-floor room and the roof, the natives of Panama build a kind of ceiling. At night people climb up a thick pole into which notches have been cut, making it serve as a ladder, and by this one reaches the strange bedroom above. Of course, these jungle dwellers have no beds, so they just stretch themselves out on old hides which are spread over the flooring of sticks—often placed so wide apart that it would be impossible to walk on them.

Whenever we watched Master clamber up these poles we envied him, for up in that primitive bedroom he was at least safe from snakes and beasts of prey which sometimes terrified us with the blood-curdling noises they made during the night.

In the low and swampy regions of Panama we saw countless crocodiles and alligators.

Before I take you further along our trail, I must tell you a very amusing story.

Upon arriving at a small settlement, a man who was dressed in white riding-breeches, elegant brown top-boots and a white sun-helmet, came to introduce himself to Master as an American sportsman, big-game-hunter and traveller.

When I looked at his spotless attire I immediately guessed that this man had never lived in places where it's really rough. However, he seemed to be a very pleasant sort of fellow, so Master chatted with him, and I didn't mind when he came to pat my neck. I was getting used to men walking around me, cocking their heads from one side to the other, staring and pointing at my head, body and legs, all the time pretending that they knew a great deal about us horses.

After a while our new acquaintance with the white riding-breeches and sun-helmet went to fetch a rifle. He asked Master to accompany him on a short shooting expedition, but when this was refused with thanks, the formidable hunter set out alone.

Master then got busy washing and otherwise attending to us and the equipment: jobs which had to be done every day, and which took some time to do thoroughly.

Suddenly we saw something come rushing through the bushes, and presently this something turned out to be our American friend, whose clothes were now very dirty. I noticed that his sun-helmet and rifle were missing, and that the man was very agitated.

Having calmed down sufficiently to speak, he gasped that he had had a terrible experience. He said that he had gone down to a swamp to shoot some alligators, and, in order to keep his feet dry, he had jumped on what he thought was a big log lying in the mud. No sooner had he landed on it than it gave a tremendous leap, flinging the would-be hunter into the slimy mud. What the poor fellow had taken for a log had turned out to be a crocodile which had been peacefully basking in the sun. When our friend realised his mistake he scrambled out of the mud and took to his heels, forgetting all about his rifle and sun-helmet which had fallen into the slime when he was pitched off the old "crock's" back.

Later on two natives accompanied the now very nervous man, and after some time the three returned with the things the great hunter had lost on his perilous expedition. Although everybody in the settlement laughed that evening, the only one who didn't seem to see the joke was our hero in the badly soiled hunting attire.

In the forests and jungles of Panama live many strange animals, some of which can be very dangerous when they are on the war-path.

The most formidable of all are the black tigers, which, however, are very rare. Jaguars, leopards, tiger-cats, wild pigs and tapirs are some of the many other animals one finds in those jungles and forests; and, of course, there are monkeys and many different kinds of birds.

Some of the monkeys are very naughty, and liked to play tricks on us. Often, when we followed a narrow trail through dense forests, we couldn't see a sign of any animal, and we thought we were the only living beings in the semi-darkness under the high, heavy roof of leaves, creepers and lichen.

Suddenly a dry twig, a big berry, or some jungle fruit would fall down, on, or near us, and presently this would be followed by another, and another.

When we looked up to see where these missiles came from, we sometimes discovered monkeys who were peeping down on us from the jungle-roof. If they were aware that we had spotted them they sometimes lost their temper, bobbing up and down, sticking out their lips and swearing at us in good monkey language, which, thank goodness, we couldn't understand.

Several times, when Master wanted some fun, he pulled out his revolver and fired a shot into the ground. When the mischievous monkeys heard the deafening noise they vanished like lightning, jumping from branch to branch. Obviously, even among these impish acrobats of the jungle, a joke's a joke.

One day, when we were nibbling the tender shoots off creepers near the place where Master had camped, he took his gun to shoot a bird to put into the pot which was hanging over the fire. A few minutes before, he had been taking some photographs, and had left his camera lying at the foot of a tree where the saddles and packs were piled up.

Some monkeys must have been watching him from above, for no sooner had he gone than a few of them came down to inspect the things. One little fellow seemed to take a fancy to the camera which he picked up to examine. He was just climbing up a creeper with his booty when Master came back and saw him. A quick shot into the air saved the treasure, for when the little thief heard the loud report, he got such a start that he dropped it, and in a flash disappeared.

Unfortunately, however, the camera fell on a thick root and was so badly damaged that it had to be repaired before it could be used again.

In these jungles and forests our progress was very slow, for in many places Master had to hack away interfering plants and creepers. The mass of twisted tree-roots over which we had to stumble, made walking very dangerous. We had to watch every step, or else our feet would have been caught in them. Even to-day I can hardly believe that we managed to cross these bad regions without a serious accident happening to one of us.

Master was lucky in finding an elderly native who offered to act as guide. Without the assistance of this plucky man we would have had great difficulty in guessing the right direction, for, to anybody but good jungle-men, all the narrow animal paths and trails look alike.

Led by our trusty guide, we penetrated into the depth of the jungles where not even Indians live, for even they avoid these unhealthy regions; only snakes and other vermin seem to thrive there.

Some of the Panamanian Indians are picturesque and interesting. They are very primitive and live but little better than animals, but yet they are not unfriendly towards white men. On festive occasions they paint their faces and bodies, and to make themselves look what they consider attractive, they file their teeth to sharp points. They dance to the beating of drums which are merely hollow bits of tree-trunks, over the ends of which hide has been fixed. These drums are beaten with the hands, the musicians squatting on the ground in a big circle, whilst the dancers hop around like crazy apes.

Like their South American cousins, these Indians are great hunters. Armed with only a spear or a bush-knife, they can kill the biggest and most ferocious jaguar or panther. To do this, a man must have very steady nerves and a quick eye, for if the hunter makes a mistake he is liable to be killed by the infuriated beast.

When hunting with spears, the natives corner a jaguar, and when he leaps at them they stick the weapon into his body, from the bottom of the neck towards the heart.

In the interior of Panama the natives prefer to hunt jaguars with bush-knives, or *machetes,* as they call them.

These men are so quick and agile that they don't mind facing these ferocious beasts afoot. Armed only with a machete, they go after a jaguar until he attacks. If a tree happens to be near, the native jumps behind it, and every time the snarling beast makes a rush for the man, he backs away, round and round the tree, slashing the big cat with his deadly machete. Jaguars are no cowards when they are fighting for their lives, and therefore, even when they have been badly wounded, they keep on attacking.

This death-dance around the tree goes on till the hunter has so weakened his prey that he can deliver the final death-blow.

Hunting jaguars with bows and arrows is much easier, though

always dangerous work. To do this, as a rule, dogs are used. When they smell a jaguar or a leopard they get very excited, and with bristling hair and wild barks follow the scent. For some strange reason even the biggest leopard or jaguar is afraid of dogs, and quickly takes refuge up a tree. As soon as the dogs are at the foot of it they bark, yelp and howl until the men arrive. When the treed beast sees its most dangerous enemies arrive, it realises that escape is almost impossible. Snarling, and showing its formidable teeth, and lashing the air with its tail, it crouches up on some stout branch, unable to decide whether to jump down and make a fight for life, or whether to remain on the tree. Having taken aim, the hunters below dispatch their wooden messengers of death. Whirring and hissing sounds end abruptly as the arrows bury themselves deep in the jaguar's lithe, muscular body.

With a roar of anger and pain the jaguar leaps high up into the air, and usually falls to the ground with a heavy thud. The dogs immediately rush at the lifeless body, and vainly try to bite through the beautiful yellow and black spotted hide.

If the jaguar still happens to be alive, terrible fights ensue, and often dogs are killed by the fell paws of these kings of the jungle, who only surrender to the greatest and undefeatable victor: Death.

.   .   .   .

Threading our way through the dense vegetation, we some-times came to open spaces in the jungle. Many of these clearings are beautiful to look at, though not nice to live in.

Enormous blue butterflies flutter from flower to flower, and

.

humming-birds dart through the leafy bushes and giant ferns.

In spite of the beauty of such places, we were glad when we moved on again, for nearly all the plants are bitter to the taste, and some are even poisonous. Jungle clearings are also the favourite haunts of slithering snakes, who go there to bask in the sun.

We had to watch very carefully where we stepped, for woe to the animal or man who disturbs one of these sleeping reptiles!

During our wanderings through these jungles and forests, we saw many ancient Indian graves which are usually covered with a big flat stone. Here and there treasure-hunters must have been busy, for many graves had been dug open.

Our guide used to tell Master many strange ghost stories, which made the jungle nights appear more mysterious and uncanny than ever.

Sometimes the deadly silence was suddenly broken by the most unearthly uproars; monkeys, wild pigs, members of the cat and dog families and hundreds of birds, roaring, snarling, barking, howling, chattering, shrieking and cackling. After a few minutes these blood-curdling outbreaks came to an end, the ensuing silence being mysterious and ghostly.

Once or twice we heard sounds like the beating of drums, which were accompanied by human voices.

When Master asked the guide where these voices came from, the grizzly old man answered that the dead jungle Indians were having a dance. According to our guide, the ghosts make merry once a month, when the moon is full.

Every now and again we came to streams and rivers which we had to cross by swimming. Sometimes this was very slow and dangerous work, and we had to be very careful to pick places where we were not likely to be attacked by hungry crocodiles and alligators.

Late one afternoon we came to a lonely hut in a jungle clearing. As we approached the primitive abode, we heard sounds of wailing and lament, which sadly contrasted with the merry song of birds whose beautifully coloured plumage vibrated in the bright sunshine.

When two big and savage-looking dogs gave the alarm an elderly man appeared. Having greeted Master and our guide, he asked them to unsaddle and make themselves at home the best they could. He apologised for not being able to offer much, for his home was a poor one, and therefore food was not plentiful. In a shaky voice he said that the cold hand of Death had descended upon his home, one of his children having been bitten by a snake. As he spoke he wiped tears off his dark and furrowed face with the back of a rough hand, and then motioned Master and the guide to follow him.

In the open hut I could see a small group of people who were squatting or kneeling in a circle around a little girl who lay on the ground on a hide. The women cried and lamented, occasionally raising their arms towards heaven, as if calling to some unseen being to help them. When the sun had set behind the high wall of trees in the jungle, a man placed lumps of animal fat into wooden bowls. Having stuck short pieces of fluffy fibre into the fat, these crude lamps were lit and placed on the mud-floor near the dead girl.

During the night, as we grazed near the hut, we could hear the wailing of the women, which sounded even more mournful when accompanied by the ugly shriek or hooting of night-birds, or the howls of prowling beasts in the darkness of the forest. Throughout the night the people stayed near the dead girl; and once or twice Master came out to sleep awhile near us.

With the coming of dawn, the dancing shadows, thrown by the flickering light of the grease candles, grew fainter and fainter.

Unaffected by the sad scenes in the humble hut, the feathered jungle musicians joyfully greeted the new day, whilst one of the men dug a hole in the ground.

Wrapped up in a cloth, the body of the child was then carried out by one of the men behind whom the other members of the family followed until they reached the edge of the tiny grave. When everybody had kissed the little girl for the last time, she was gently lowered to her resting-place, and covered with a heavy blanket of black earth.

Some of the men then shook clenched fists at the jungle whilst the tearful women called upon heaven for consolation and justice.

As on many former occasions, we were glad when we were on our way again. For the next two or three days we watched every step, but as we saw no signs of snakes we soon became careless again. We merely wondered where and when we would get our next meal, for familiarity breeds contempt; and an empty stomach knows no caution.

Not only we horses, but also Master had to eat strange things sometimes. Off and on he shot wood-pigeons and wild turkeys, of which he seemed to be very fond. In some regions he wasn't so lucky, and had to eat whatever he could find or kill. Since the natives in certain parts of South and Central America call strange things "delicacies," Master even had to eat big lizards, armadillo, wild pig, strange frogs and toads, and once even snake. Incidentally, he seemed to like it, for I saw him take a second helping.

Once he was so hungry that he had to shoot monkeys, which he cut up and boiled with the roots of a plant called *yucca* or *mandioca.*

Having travelled through dense jungle for many days, we came to a high mountain which was very difficult to climb. Up in the heights it was bitterly cold, and as we looked down, the jungle-roof in the distance looked like a rolling prairie.

The mountain was so steep, and the ground so slippery, that we often fell. Master and the guide hacked steps for us, and sometimes they even helped us by pushing from behind.

The sudden change from the steaming jungles to this icy atmosphere made us feel almost ill, but luckily we only spent one night on this mountain from where we could see both the Atlantic and the Pacific Oceans.

The down-hill journey was even worse than the climb had been, and, to make things more unpleasant, a terrific storm broke out, the icy sleet and rain seeming to penetrate to our very bones. Even at midday it was almost dark, and lightning, like blinding sheets of flame, flashed through the black clouds near us, making them look as if they were on fire, the accompanying thunder being so terrific that the very rocks shook and trembled.

Unable to find shelter anywhere, we slid and stumbled towards the valley where we knew we would be safe.

The fury of the storm subsided when we reached the timber line where we spent the night as best we could, continuing our down-hill journey until we came to a valley where we saw several huts, green fields and cattle. We had reached civilisation once more!—The Panamanian jungles were conquered! A few days later our excellent guide left us to return to his distant home. Master gave him money, a rifle and clothes: rewards the good man fully deserved, for he had worked very hard and had suffered a great deal without ever complaining or grumbling.

"Good-bye, grizzly old jungle-man! Hope to see you again!"

.   .   .   .

The country we were in now is a Central American republic called Costa Rica, where some of the best coffee in the world is grown.

The coffee-plant looks rather like a laurel-tree with small white flowers. When the fruits are ripe they are about the size and colour of small dark-red cherries. In each fleshy fruit are embedded two hard, greenish seeds, which are taken out and roasted until they are dark brown, and have the aroma men are so fond of.

STORY TWENTY

Master is accidentally locked up in a jail. Another short sea journey. A hold-up. Volcanoes, forests and lakes. Mancha gives a stranger a riding lesson. Good-bye, Central America!

ONCE we were back in inhabited parts, travelling was easy, for though the roads were very rough, they were good for us to trot on.

We passed through several villages which were none too clean. Besides coffee, all sorts of tropical fruits are grown in Costa Rica—chiefly bananas and oranges.

When we spent the night in villages where there were no hotels or even dirty inns, Master always had to sleep in the police-station, the jail being the only available bed-room. If prisoners happened to be in these filthy dungeons, they were put into stocks for the night.

Master used to sweep out a corner, and there spread his blankets over which he sprinkled insect-powder, of which he always carried a supply.

If the police-station had a back yard, we were put into it, but if there wasn't such a place, we just stood outside the tumble-down shacks where our fodder was thrown on the ground.

One evening, after a long march through stifling heat, we arrived at one of these dismal villages where Master finally found the "jefe de policia" (chief of police). Although the dusky gentleman was drunk, he was very polite, and showed us the way to the jail. When we came to a heavily barred door in which there was an opening that was just big enough for a man to stick his head through, the *jefe de policia* stopped, and, producing a huge key, opened the door which made a noise like a squealing pig.

Whilst Master took the pack and saddles off us, the drunken chief of police staggered away.

Having carried all our belongings into the jail, Master locked the door from the outside, and then took us to a stream, where we drank while he washed us. After this treat he took us back to the police-station, and then went to see if anybody would sell him some fodder—a job which wasn't always easy, and sometimes meant going from one shack to another.

Having bought a heap of dry corn-stalks, he went to see if anybody would cook something for him. This usually meant another tramp from door to door till some old woman prepared him a portion of boiled rice, maize, fried bananas or eggs, which he often ate whilst sitting on the pack to be near us.

On this occasion he had just gone into the jail to fetch out his saddle to sit on, when the now very wobbly *jefe de policia* came staggering past the place. When the local tin god saw that the door of his prison was wide open, and the key sticking in the lock, he closed it with a bang; and before Master realised what was happening, he was locked up, and the chief of police was swaying away; most likely to see where he could find another drink of sugar-cane brandy. Master stuck his head through the opening in the door, and in vain yelled after the tipsy official, who went shuffling round a corner, the huge key dangling from one of his fingers.

Although we felt sorry for poor Master, we couldn't help laughing when we saw his head stick out through the iron bars of the prison door, calling and whistling till we thought he'd blow out his front teeth.

At last an inquisitive boy came to see who might be this red-haired and freckled jail-bird, and presently several more dark and half-naked children collected outside. However, in spite of Master's promises and threats, none of the kids moved to call the chief of police who by this time, must have been fast asleep in some hut.

Half the kids and skinny dogs of the village had assembled outside the *calabozo* when the older generation began to wonder if a revolution had broken out. Men and women came hurrying towards the jail, out of which Master peeped like a fox out of his burrow.

Even the starved mongrels realised that something was wrong, and guessing that Master was the cause of all this commotion, they barked, growled, yelped and snarled, the bravest even rushing at the jail door to bite the stout iron bars and knobs with which it was re-enforced.

After a while Master managed to explain what had happened. Although his story was not believed, a few men went to look for the *jefe de policia* who, supported by the strong arm of a native, came staggering through the crowd.

Even the animated skeletons of dogs seemed to realise the great importance of the drunken man, for when he appeared they slunk away with their tails between their legs. Possibly the poor wretches had no desire to renew their acquaintance with his heavy sandals, which, no doubt, had caused them rude and painful awakenings when they had happened to be slumbering near a wall on the shady side of the street.

A few minutes after Master had been released, the crowd dispersed. Nobody, excepting ourselves, saw the joke; in fact, some of the men seemed to be disappointed that no revolution had broken out; for besides drinking, watching cock, and bull-fights, and listening to political speeches, revolutions offer the only opportunities to make these people feel that they are really alive.

The next Central American republic through which we should have passed is called Nicaragua, but as the place was over-run by all sorts of armies who were fighting against each other—most of them not even knowing why they were enemies—Master took us down to a small port on the Pacific Ocean, and there loaded us on to a ship.

This wasn't as easy and simple as it sounds, for the coast is so shallow that big boats have to anchor out at sea, and therefore, to reach them, we had to be taken out on a flat barge. First of all a carpenter had to make two very strong crates for us, and when we had been boxed up in them, a crowd of fussing and yelling natives lifted us on to the barge. Luckily Master was there to help, for if he hadn't told the men what to do, they would have dropped us into the shark-infested sea.

Safely on the barge, we were taken out to the big ship which seemed to become higher and larger as we approached. Thick ropes were then put around our crates, and presently a crane hoisted us high up into the air. I was so nervous that I couldn't even move, so I just stood still, trembling and holding my breath. Suddenly I felt a gentle bump, and when I looked around me I saw that I was on the deck of a ship.

After a while Master appeared with some fodder, which made us forget the fright we had had, and then the ship began to throb, and I noticed that we were moving. The golden sands of the shore, the foaming surf, and the palm-trees seemed to be moving away from us, until the land we had just left looked like a dark-green line on the hazy bluish-green horizon of the Pacific Ocean.

We had only been on board for one night when we came to a small port where we were unloaded without accident.

Resuming the journey, we passed through several villages and small towns, all of which were about the same: dirty and uninteresting.

The country we were in is called San Salvador.

During the heat of the day most of the people sleep in hammocks, which are slung between two posts in the usually very untidy huts.

A revolution was brewing in this tiny republic, and therefore, army detachments were stationed here and there.

One evening we were held up by some dusky soldiers who were clad in filthy and tattered uniforms. One of the men—who was either a corporal or a general—pulled out a rusty old sword, and barked at Master to surrender in the name of the law.

As the circle of soldiers closed in on us, I lifted a hind-leg to make them keep at a respectful distance, and when I saw the fat and stocky commander I felt like giving him a good nip in a soft place.

Master had quite an argument with this man who seemed to be getting more and more excited when a crowd of curious and unkempt people collected to see what all this fuss was about.

When Master realised that words were of no avail, he opened the saddle-bags and took from them his passport, which he held out to the commander. Obviously the *comandante* wasn't much of a scholar, for it took him a long time to spell out the words, whilst the soldiers and bystanders with open mouths listened and stared with black slit eyes.

Having struggled through the contents of the document, the manners of the *comandante* changed completely. In a harsh voice he ordered his soldiers and the crowd to retire, and when he turned to Master he was so polite that I thought he was trying to sell him his old sword which he still held in his hand.

The now very embarrassed man apologised for the trouble, inconvenience and delay he had caused us, and explained that he had taken Master for a fleeing revolutionary general.

Our companion at once seized the opportunity and asked the commander to order some of his men to find fodder for us; a wish that was immediately granted. Within half an hour a big heap of grass lay before us, and while we filled our empty stomachs we watched Master who squatted near us, giving all his attention to a wooden bowl which was filled with steaming beans and boiled rice.

What a pity he wasn't more often taken for a revolutionary general!

In San Salvador we saw several volcanoes and some beautiful lakes, but we were glad when we came to the border of the next republic: Guatemala. We were in higher regions now, and therefore it was not so hot and sticky.

The natives in these parts are very fond of playing music on strange instruments called *marimbas*. They look like tables on which there are many pieces of hard-wood, arranged like the keys of a piano. When these bits of wood are struck with small hammers, a strange kind of music is produced.

We hadn't gone far into Guatemala when we came to mountainous country, and soon we were in regions where the climate was cool and agreeable, and where the vegetation was no longer tropical. Instead of palms and creepers, there were forests of fir-trees, and many of the hills were covered with sweet grasses and lovely wild flowers.

We jogged over fairly good roads until we arrived at Guatemala City—the capital of the republic—where we had a good rest and plenty of excellent fodder.

In a nice stable we made the best of our holiday, sleeping on soft beds of straw, which many a time we would have gobbled up with glee when we were out in the wilds with nothing to eat.

Every day Master took us out for a little exercise, but as he took no pack with him, only one of us was saddled up, the other following behind until a change-over was made.

Many people used to visit us at the stable, but as we didn't like strangers, we weren't very polite and friendly with them. We didn't mind being looked at from a distance, but when some of the strangers had the impertinence to enter the big loose-box we were in, we very soon chased them out. All we had to do was to lay back our ears and look vicious, and pretend to be about to bite the intruders, and they would retire as quickly as they could.

One morning, just as we were about to leave the stable to go out for our daily exercise, a man in uniform came to speak to Master. During the conversation I heard the stranger ask if he might have a short ride on Mancha. I understood Master to tell the man that neither my pal nor I were used to being handled by anybody but himself, and that there would be trouble if a stranger tried to ride us.

On hearing this conversation I pricked up my ears and listened, for it sounded as if we were about to have some fun.

The man bragged so much about what he had done and could do on a horse, that Master finally gave in and told him to please himself.

When Master had carefully tightened Mancha's girth, he handed him over to the stranger who hadn't even the decency to introduce himself to my pal. Mancha had a wicked twinkle in his eye. Instead of being polite, the man tried to pull him along by the bridle, and when Mancha refused to move, the would-be rider made some very insulting remarks about him.

Realising that my pal wouldn't follow him, the man decided to mount; but as stubborn Mancha refused to stand still he flicked him in the flank with his riding-whip, annoying the old boy so much that he snorted and gave a kick into the air, where-upon Master went to hold his head until the stranger had scrambled into the saddle. Mancha stood stock-still for a moment, and when I caught his eye he gave me one of his mean-ing winks. Just then the man dug his spurs into Mancha's ribs, at the same time making a chucking noise with his mouth. This made my pal so mad, and gave him such a start that he went off like a rocket. To show that he wasn't dumb and stupid, he squealed and grunted, at the same time putting his head between his fore-legs. If Mancha had wanted to, he could have sent the stranger flying with one good buck, but he disliked him so much that he decided to give him a good shaking-up first. For a few seconds—which must have seemed like hours to the poor creature on his back—he skipped about and bucked furiously. Having done enough of this, he jumped into the air as high as he could, at the same time arching his back like a cat. This sent the dusky "caballero" flying and turning somersaults, until he landed on the ground like a bale of hay. When he got up he was so white in the face that one of the bystanders ran to fetch a glass of brandy which put new life into the great rider who soon disappeared, calling us all sorts of names which I dare not repeat.

.   .   .   .

Master had to be very careful to keep our hoofs in good order. In swampy regions they were apt to become very soft, and when we came to parts where we had to walk on sharp rocks, gravel and stones, our hoofs would have cracked if they hadn't been greased and otherwise attended to.

Of course, we wore shoes all the time, for without this protection no horse could travel through damp and dry regions. When we were wild we didn't need shoes, but you must bear in mind that we lived where there were no swamps to soften our hoofs, and therefore they were tough and hard, and we could gallop over stones and gravel without getting sore feet.

Master always carried a supply of horse-shoes in his saddle-bags, and often, when we were out in the wilds, he had to tack new shoes on us. If we happened to be passing through a place where there was a blacksmith, Master always let him do this job, which is not at all an easy one. To shoe a horse well requires much practice and skill, for if a mistake is made, and a nail is driven into the quick—as the soft part of the hoof is called—it can easily cripple him.

This I found out shortly after we left Guatemala, for while we rested in this stable, a horse-shoer accidentally drove a nail too near to the quick of one of my hoofs.

At first I didn't feel anything, but later it began to hurt, and after a few days the pain became almost unbearable.

I'll tell you more about this later, when we come to the part where I became very ill and nearly died.

.   .   .   .

When we left Guatemala City we felt so fit and strong that we wanted to trot and canter, but as Master wouldn't let us do this, we just jogged along at a merry gait.

The country through which we passed is very beautiful, and the climate cool and healthy. Our trail led over mountains and hills which were covered with forests, and we passed high volcanoes which sometimes break out in violent eruptions, destroying the picturesque Indian villages and settlements for miles around.

In the highland of Guatemala there are some beautiful lakes near which different Indian tribes cultivate their fields.

Some of these Indians will not allow white men to stay in their villages after the sun has set. In the day-time the presence of white people doesn't seem to annoy them, but woe to the pale-face who tries to remain among these natives when the shadows of night begin to fall!

Like most Indians, the natives of Guatemala are fond of music and dancing. Flutes, drums and *marimbas* are their favourite instruments, and their dances are often grotesque, though merry affairs.

Many centuries ago, a powerful nation of Indians—called *Mayas*—lived in parts of what is now called Guatemala and Yucatan. The Mayas have died out long ago, but to this day one can see the ruins of the temples and strange monuments they had built. Rocks and stones were shaped into horrible monsters and snakes, and high pyramids were adorned with stone heads of dragons, lions and demons which were adored or feared by the ancient Mayas who even sacrificed human beings to their gods.

Continuing our march over mountains and through fertile valleys, we once more approached the Pacific Ocean.

One morning, after we had followed a good trail which led up a mountain, we reached the top from where we had a marvellous view.

To the west, at our feet, we could faintly see the glittering vastness of the Pacific Ocean. The mountain range, on which we were, extended towards the north and south as far as we could see, and between us and the ocean were the slopes of the mountain; barren at the top, and green and greener in the lower regions where the tropical mists acted like a greyish-purple veil which hid the low-land from our view. Quite near us a volcano towered high into the deep blue sky, its scarred precipitous walls and smokeless crater seeming to wait for the next eruption.

More than once we heard natives tell Master strange stories about volcanoes in which—according to one tale—live wicked giants, devils and dragons who sometimes fight to the death. On such occasions the ground rocks and trembles, and loud rumblings and thunder are heard under the ground where these terrific fights take place. The huge dragons spit out so much fire and smoke that the tops of the mountains are blown high into the sky, killing men and animals who have the misfortune to be living near these subterranean battle-grounds.

In spite of these awe-inspiring tales, we enjoyed the cool breezes which played with our manes and tails, and we never even bothered to wonder what would have happened to us if a war of giants and dragons had started when we were quite near some of these entrances to the mysterious underworld.

What really interested us were the green patches on the slopes below us, for we knew that there we could find something to eat, and we were happy when Master guided us towards them.

As we were winding our way down the steep and rocky trail, I began to feel a pain in one of my hoofs. With the passing of hours this pain became more and more acute, but in spite of this I continued.

By evening we had reached the warm regions where we halted at a solitary hut.

My hoof hurt me so much that I passed the whole night fighting off mosquitoes, never sleeping a wink.

Early in the morning Master came to take us to water, and as we went towards the stream which came bubbling down the mountain, he noticed that I was very lame, and at once examined my foot, which I lifted for him to look at.

Had I been able to speak, I could have told him what was wrong, but as it was I had to let him discover the cause of the trouble for himself.

In spite of the pain I suffered, I was obliged to hobble along for two days, but as we travelled slowly and rested often, I managed to get along.

At the foot of the mountain we came to a river, and when we had crossed it we were no longer in Guatemala, but in Mexico. Several men who wore huge broad-brimmed hats, and had revolvers in their belts, came to greet us, and made a great fuss of Master, who told them that I was ill.

These men—who were Mexican border-guards—at once made ready to escort us to a village which was some miles away. To make walking easier for me they relieved me of the pack and saddle which were loaded on one of their mules.

Painfully, and very slowly I then hobbled along, until quite exhausted, I arrived at a village where Mancha and I were put into a shed in the back-yard of a dirty house which people there called an "hotel."

Assisted by a man, Master at once began to operate on my foot. With a sharp knife he cut away the thick horny sole of my bad hoof till he came to the source of the trouble. As soon as he had started to cut into the quick, a lot of matter squirted out, and I immediately felt a great relief. While he was cutting away and disinfected the inflamed parts, I never moved, for although it hurt, I knew that he did it for my good.

When the operation was finished, my foot was bandaged up with so much cloth that it looked like a big ball. Slowly and gingerly I put my foot to the ground, and finding that it didn't hurt as it had done before, I gradually put more and more weight on it.

Mancha was tethered quite near me, and he was so

sympathetic that I almost forgot my troubles.

When Master brought a pile of fodder, and a sack of corn and bran, we guessed that he intended to stay in this village for some time. This was wise on his part, for even if I had tried, I couldn't have walked a hundred yards. Thinking over the situation, I was afraid that I would be left behind, or perhaps, be sold to the first willing buyer.

As I've said before, the cause of all my pain and trouble was a nail which had been driven too near the quick by a horse-shoer in Guatemala City.

Instead of getting rid of me, Master made my stall comfortable, and whenever I suffered, he helped me as much as he could.

With the passing of time, and with all the doctoring and care, I got better and better until I was well enough to be taken for short walks to loosen my stiff limbs.

I had almost completely recovered when—late one night—a traveller arrived with a mule. Before Master had retired for the night, he had placed a lot of fodder before us. This he always bought from men who brought it into the village on donkeys. Grass was only sold during the day-time, so he always took good care to buy a big supply to last us throughout the night.

When the traveller and his mule arrived it was too late to buy grass, so the stranger simply tied his animal alongside me, knowing fully well that it would help itself to my fodder.

Even before the man had reached the door of the house, his hungry mule tried to push me aside, and when I mildly objected to such treatment and greed, the nasty beast gave me a vicious bite in the neck. I wish that Mancha had been in my place, for I'm sure he would very soon have taught it manners. I wasn't strong enough to do more than protest, but my remarks were entirely lost on that greedy mule, which ate so fast that I thought it would choke.

After a while my unwelcome visitor seemed to think that I had no business to be where I was, for whenever I tried to eat I was pushed away, and even bitten. This sort of thing went on till I began to get really annoyed, and decided to show who was the owner of the fodder.

Accordingly, the next time the mule got nasty, I gave it a good bite, which made it so mad that it turned round and kicked me with all its might. I wasn't able to defend myself as I could have done before my illness, so the fight that ensued was very one-sided, and when it was all over I was so weak that I could hardly stand. My body was bruised and bleeding where the mule's sharp shoes had cut through my hide; and, worst of all, one of my knees was severely injured.

Long before daybreak the owner of the mule came to saddle up, and when Master appeared to say "Good morning" to us, the two nasty strangers were miles away from the village.

My wounds were immediately washed and attended to, but in spite of all the care I received, my knee got worse, until, after a few days, I could hardly stand on the terribly swollen leg. When I lay down to rest I couldn't get up unless Master, with the assistance of friends, helped me to rise. With the passing of days, my condition became more and more serious, and I was such a wreck that I heard people tell Master to kill me.

I had been suffering agonies for three or four weeks, when, one morning, Master and several of his new friends came towards me. I noticed that they brought with them two long poles and pieces of canvas which looked like girths. When Master had put two of these strips of canvas under my body, the poles were passed through them. Four men then supported me—two in front and two behind—and slowly helped me out into the hot, sandy street.

Mancha was left in his stall from where he called to me desperately, for this was the first time that we had been parted since we had made friends in Patagonia. Whenever I heard my dear pal's voice I answered; but as I hobbled away, his calls became fainter and fainter, until I could hear them no longer.

Master, who kept on patting and fondling me, looked so sad that I thought I was being taken away to be killed; but I felt so miserable and ill that I didn't care.

To my surprise we came to a railway station, where I was loaded on a wagon in which a soft bed of straw had been prepared for me. I heard Master tell a man to look after me well, and I noticed that he gave him some money.

I was still calling Mancha; but the only reply I got was a shrill whistle from the engine, whereupon Master hurriedly hugged my head and then jumped off the wagon, which had already started to move.

I was on the train for four long days and nights. To tell you what I thought and felt during this long journey would be impossible.

At first it was very hot, and thousands of insects pestered me, but later the train began to climb up-hill, and soon the air became cooler and more agreeable.

The man who was with me looked after me very well, and

whenever the train stopped he brought me water to quench my thirst.

On the fourth day I was taken off the train with great care, and when I looked about me I was amazed to see that I was in what appeared to be a big town. A number of people came to stare at me, and to my surprise several photographers pointed their cameras in my direction. What could be the meaning of all this? Surely nobody could possibly take an interest in a poor crippled horse?

Several men helped to load me on a motor-truck, whereupon I was driven to a stable where many willing hands assisted me into a stall; here I lay down on a soft bed of straw.

Two veterinary surgeons examined me carefully; and when they had finished they shook their heads. Although I heard them tell a bystander that it would be kind to put me out of my misery, I didn't mind, for besides being in great pain and feeling very weak, I had lost the company of the two beings I liked best in this world.

An hour or two passed, and then a Japanese gentleman came to examine me. Having done this very thoroughly, he turned to the same bystander the two veterinary surgeons had spoken to and said that he thought he could cure me.

This Japanese was so good and clever that my health soon improved; and at the end of two weeks I was able to stand on my legs.

Everybody was so good to me, and the fodder I ate so excellent that I regained strength and spirits; but in spite of this I couldn't forget my two pals who—by this time—must have been far, far away from me.

M

After several weeks I was so fit that I was even saddled up and taken for a canter in a beautiful park.

The city I was in is called Mexico City, and is the capital of the big republic of Mexico.

One day, when I least expected it, I had the greatest and most pleasant surprise in my life. However, you'll hear about this later. Now it is Mancha's turn to tell you what he did after I was taken away from him

STORY TWENTY-ONE

*Mancha's adventures and travels until he was re-united
with Gato*

I DIDN'T know what had become of Gato; for, about two long
hours after I had seen him hobble away, Master returned all
alone. I called and called, but although I pricked up my ears
and listened intently, I got no reply. I was glad to have Master
near me, for if I had been left all alone I would have been feeling very miserable and lonely.

When he brought out the saddles and got busy greasing the
leather and straps, I guessed that he was making preparations
to leave the village. I still hoped that Gato would return, and I
was looking forward to being out in the open with him.

Towards evening Master left me. He was away for an unusually long time, and I wondered what he might be doing.
After a long spell of waiting I heard the clatter of hoofs which
seemed to be coming towards the yard I was in. Thinking that
it was Gato, my heart beat with joy; but when the gate swung
open I could hardly believe my eyes. Instead of coming with
my pal, Master led in a horse I had never seen before, and a few
moments later a man arrived with a nice-looking mare.

Much as I tried, I simply couldn't make out the meaning of
all this; but when I saw Master hand over some money to the
man, I guessed that he had bought the two animals.

I was so interested in what was going on that I forgot my

disappointment at not seeing Gato, and when Master tied the two horses in the stall near me, and introduced us to each other, I thought I must be dreaming.

Very early next morning, a man who wore a huge straw hat, arrived. Having saddled up the two horses and myself, Master mounted on me, and the stranger jumped on one of my new acquaintances. The mare carried the pack, the sight and smell of which brought back memories of Gato.

However, I had no time for sad thoughts, for as soon as the stranger with the big straw hat had mounted, he led the way out of the yard and trotted down a sandy street.

I very soon came to the conclusion that this man was our guide, because, as soon as we had left the village behind us, he led the way into a forest which was almost a jungle.

For a day or two we followed a path which wound through the dense vegetation, but later we entered swampy regions where progress was slow and difficult.

By this time I had made friends with the two horses, and the three of us got on pretty well.

Even though the weather seemed to have conspired against us, we forged our way through low and unhealthy regions where we had to swim across many deep rivers and evil-smelling swampy pools.

Torrential rains fell every day, and for long stretches the mud and slime were so deep that we sank in up to our bellies.

The two horses who had joined us were born and raised in low coastal regions, and therefore were accustomed to all the tricks and dangers of swamps. Both were good swimmers, especially the mare, whom I greatly envied. When she swam, her back rarely got wet, and she cut through the water with the speed and ease of an Indian canoe.

Every now and again we came to clearings in the jungle and forest; and, if people lived there, Master and the guide slept in the primitive one-roomed huts.

I often watched men and women prepare food for themselves. If I told you about all the strange things I have seen human beings eat you would, perhaps, not believe me. Off and on I've heard people say that a man had "the stomach of a horse." If they had said "the stomach of a man," it would have been more to the point, for if we horses tried to eat all the nasty things men stuff themselves with, we'd die.

I only know one animal which can beat men at eating strange things; and that's the ostrich. These birds can swallow broken glass, pocket-knives, flowers, whole oranges, big horny beetles, and many other things which would make me very ill. But when I think back, and remember what I've seen men eat and drink, I'm sure that they are not far behind the greediest ostrich. No wonder your doctors have to be clever to keep you alive!

Some of the jungle forests along the Southern Pacific coast of Mexico are very beautiful to look at, though far from easy and pleasant to travel through.

Big, bright-red and blue macaws flew over our heads, and ugly black monkeys looked at us from the tops of trees. Some of these bad-tempered creatures seemed to resent our presence, and expressed their disapproval by showing their big yellow teeth while bobbing up and down and viciously shaking the branches they stood on, and at the same time snarling and spitting at us.

Many of the streams and pools are infested with alligators, and the dense jungles are the favourite haunts of jaguars and other prowlers.

By this time, experience had taught me that men can do many clever things, and that they are able to dominate animals which are much stronger than they.

I knew that men could lasso horses and cattle, but I would never have believed that some human beings are so daring and cunning that they can lasso crocodiles under water. This may sound like a tall Patagonian story to you, but I saw it being done, so you may please yourself, and believe me or not.

In a small village where we were staying, Master was talking to a group of men. After a while, accompanied by a number of villagers who were mounted on mules and donkeys, we followed a track which led towards a slow-flowing river where we halted. As it was shortly after noon, the sun was very hot, and all the animals and birds seemed to be asleep, excepting crickets who chirruped so loudly that the vibrating noise was jarring to the ear.

When all the men had dismounted, and their animals were tied to some bushes, they went to the river bank where one of them undressed. He was a sturdy, dark Mexican, who looked fine as he stood naked in the strong sun which showed his muscles to full advantage.

Taking a lasso in his hand, he slowly walked along the bank, every now and again stopping to stare into the water below him. Most of the men—who quietly followed behind him—were armed with heavy clubs and bush-knives, which made me wonder what was going to happen.

Suddenly the naked man gave a signal, and having handed one end of the lasso to two or three of his followers, he coiled up the other end of the rope in his hand, whereupon he noiselessly slid into the water, and immediately disappeared below the surface.

Suspecting that crocodiles were in this river, I held my breath, for surely the man was in danger of being torn to pieces by these dangerous reptiles.

It seemed as if five minutes must have passed since the man had disappeared; and still the only sign of him was an occasional bubble which rose to the surface of the water near the bank where the other men and Master waited in silence.

Presently the swimmer's head and shoulders appeared. Having taken a deep breath, the man hurriedly scrambled up the bank, whereupon the men pulled in the rope as fast as they could. I guessed that something heavy must be at the submerged end, for the men yelled with joy, as if they had caught a big fish.

Soon there was a terrible commotion in the water which foamed, splashed and seethed as a huge crocodile came to the surface. Whilst some pulled in the lasso, others danced about, excitedly swinging their clubs and *machetes*. When the struggling crocodile had been pulled on dry land, it lashed about its huge tail and viciously snapped its formidable jaws, but in spite of the terrific fight the monster put up, it was finally killed.

While the brave swimmer told Master how he had lassoed the reptile under water, some of the men cut open the dead animal, and took from it some fat; this the natives in many parts of South and Central America use as a remedy for rheumatism and other ailments.

It appears that crocodiles have caves under the river banks, and that the entrances to these layers are always below the surface of the water. When the sun is hot, the ugly reptiles often sleep in these entrances; and that's the time when they can be lassoed.

According to the Mexican who spoke to Master, crocodiles never attack a man if he swims under water, and when they sleep, they love to have their bodies scratched under the fore-legs where the skin is thin and soft. Whilst giving the old "crock" this last treat, the rope is tied round one leg, whereupon the man quickly comes to the surface, which is the signal for his friends on the bank to pull.

It all sounded so easy when the man explained how he performed the dangerous and seemingly impossible trick; but I had no doubt that Master would take good care never to have occasion to use this fearless native's advice.

Rumours that a revolution had broken out reached us when we were in the wilds; and as we came nearer the more inhabited parts, it was obvious that we would soon be mixed up in the trouble. Bandits had already started to make travelling very unsafe, and we had a first taste of what their activities can mean when we were shot at from an ambush. Luckily, however, the bullets went wide of their mark, excepting one, which ripped a hole in the sheep-skin on my saddle.

We managed to get away safely, but we hadn't gone far when we came to a solitary hut which had been raided by these ruthless bandits. Not satisfied with stealing everything the poor settler possessed, the outlaws had killed one of the men, and before disappearing into the forest they had set the hut on fire.

When we arrived on this scene of sorrow and desolation, the weeping women implored Master to help them, but as this was impossible he promised to inform the authorities about the happenings, whereupon we immediately continued our hazardous journey.

Without further incident we reached a village where Master at once made a report to the commander of an army detachment which was stationed there. Hearing that the regions we had to cross were overrun by bandits and revolutionary troops, our guide refused to accompany us further, and decided to return home where his wife must be worrying about his safety.

I didn't like the look of things, for I doubted that we would be able to go far without getting into serious trouble.

When we left the village we were accompanied by a strong escort of cavalry. Every man was armed to the teeth and ready to shoot, for it would have been easy to ambush us in the dense forests through which we slowly advanced in single file.

On reaching the next place where soldiers were stationed, our escort was relieved by a new one whose duty it was to see us safely to the next army detachment.

Owing to the swampy nature of the country, our progress was very slow; and to make things more difficult, we had to do a lot of swimming, which was very troublesome, because some of the horses and soldiers weren't used to it.

During one of our weary marches we were told that bandits were camping in a hollow near a river. Our attack was so sudden and unexpected that we caught two men, who were immediately hanged on a tree. To serve other outlaws as a warning, the two dead bandits were left dangling from a branch; and as we jogged away, the black buzzards who had been flying above our heads, circled down, lower and lower.

I was thankful when we came out of the hot and swampy regions, and when I once more trod on hard dry land.

The next escort took us towards some high mountains where the trails soon became very rough and difficult. We were obliged to cross several wide and turbulent rivers, which was all the more exciting work because only a few of the soldiers could swim. Their horses, too, weren't very strong, and therefore, after a few days, most of them had to be left behind, to be picked up on the escort's return journey.

Being left without their horses, the soldiers were obliged to go afoot, but what with long marches and bad trails, their feet were soon so sore that they could hardly stand on them.

In different Indian settlements, our cripples commandeered donkeys which had to do the walking for them.

Whenever I remember the sad and yet comical procession which threaded its way over high mountains and through deep canyons, I can't help laughing.

Some of the shaggy little donkeys were so scraggy that their spines stuck out like miniature mountain ranges, and their ribs reminded me of the *marimbas* on which the Guatemalan Indians play music.

Since the foot-sore members of our escort had no saddles to fit on these tiny, but very strong donkeys, they had to ride with just a blanket under their seats. After a day or two of being bumped and jolted about on these uncomfortable donkeys, the poor riders were so sore and stiff that they couldn't decide which position was the worst: standing, sitting or lying down!

In spite of their discomforts, to which the lack of food and water was sometimes added, they carried on without uttering · more complaints than occasional groans of agony. Believe me, friends, these Mexicans were real heroes; and although their uniforms were in rags, and their heavy sandals stained black with sweat and dust, they were fine soldiers.

In parts where revolutionary troops were active we had to make our marches at night. In mountainous regions, where the narrow trails often led past deep precipices, this was hard and dangerous work.

For days and nights we pushed ahead until we came to a vast

A trail in the Mexican *sierras* (mountains)

high plain. As far as I could see, the sandy table-land was covered with patches of bush and gigantic cactus plants, and in the far distance glittered the snow-capped peaks of mountains and volcanoes.

Many members of our escort were so tired and sore that we could only travel very slowly; so when we came to a town, Master told them that he would prefer to go on alone with me.

The poor soldiers weren't sorry to hear this, for most of them needed a rest to get over their soreness, and to give their blistered feet as chance to heal.

In spite of the revolution and bandits, Master and I continued our northward journey. We saw many interesting things and picturesque Indians with their huge hats.

Gradually we came to more inhabited parts where people were very kind to us. In villages and towns, bands played when we arrived; and in one or two places they even rang the church bells. Sometimes the men were so pleased to meet us that they celebrated by drinking too much. On several occasions this led to incidents, some of which were very funny.

The mayor of one village insisted on racing his horse against me, and although Master kept on telling the good man that I'm not a race-horse, the mayor persisted until Master gave in.

The village grandee was so drunk that I was amazed to see that he was still able to climb into the saddle of his prancing horse—a fine-looking Mexican mustang. Waving an arm, the mayor announced that the race was to be run once round the *plaza,* or square, and that the winner would be declared *campeón mundial* (world's champion).

On hearing this, I nearly burst out laughing, but when I looked at the rough cobblestones with which the square was paved I became nervous, for I realised how dangerous and foolish it was to race over them.

Master tried his best to make the mayor give up the idea of matching his horse against me, but by this time the crowd was keen to see the *carrera,* as a race is called in Spanish. When we were ready, the signal for the start was given, and the mayor's fleet mount started off with the speed of an arrow leaving a bow. By the time I got going, my rival was three or four lengths ahead of me, racing hell for leather. As we dashed along, our hoofs clattered on the hard cobble-stones, making sparks fly like in a blacksmith's shop when a red-hot iron is being hammered into shape.

Going at top speed we shot towards the first corner where we had to turn round a hat which had been placed on the ground.

The mayor was so keen to win the race that he didn't slow down his horse before turning the sharp corner; and in consequence his animal slipped and fell, sending the rider head first through the door of a house. When I saw this and heard the crash, I thought the poor man was killed, but by the time I had come to a standstill the mayor was on his feet, staggering after his horse which now bolted out of the village. Several riders who had been watching the crazy race dashed after the fugitive, while the would-be *campeón mundial* rubbed his head—on which alcohol seemed to have had more effect than the now shattered door.

Shortly after we had left the mountains of Southern Mexico behind us, Master was so ill with malaria that he could hardly ride; but in spite of this we pushed ahead every day. The fever made him feel hot and cold in turns, and sometimes he shivered so violently that the blanket he was wrapped up in moved as if he were tittering and chuckling to himself under it. Fortunately we were now on a plain where travelling was easy, and soon we came to parts where the villages were fairly close together.

Heading towards two beautiful mountains which were covered with snow, we came to a big town where a doctor attended to Master, who by this time, was a regular wreck. Instead of taking a good rest, of which he was in sore need, he set out again after two days. Somehow I felt that something out-of-the-way was about to happen soon, for although my sick friend wasn't fit to ride, he made two very long journeys.

It felt strange to trot on a good road, for since we had left Guatemala City—now hundreds of miles away—we had only travelled over rough trails, and often through parts where not even a footpath was to be found.

Every now and again motor-cars passed us; and I was surprised to see the occupants greet us joyously, as if they were friends. What puzzled me most was to hear Master hum tunes to himself, for he was still ill, and surely he couldn't be in a merry mood.

Later in the day an aeroplane circled over our heads, and presently many men who wore uniforms, and who were riding on noisy motor-cycles, stopped while their leader spoke to Master.

Soon after I heard the drumming of many hoofs, and within a few minutes we were surrounded by a large crowd of cheering riders, who were dressed in colourful and glittering costumes of Mexican cowboys, or *charros*, as they are called. There was such a commotion and so much noise that I thought we were being attacked, and I was just about to start biting and kicking when I thought I was seeing a vision.

Charro

Master must have seen it at the same time, for he jumped out of the saddle and, as the vision came closer, rushed towards it—and threw his arms around Gato's sturdy neck!

It took me several seconds to believe my eyes, and when I was sure that I wasn't dreaming I stepped forward to sniff Gato's nose and to nicker a heart-felt "How are you, dear old pal?"

The crowd around us made such a noise, and we were being pushed so much that I couldn't say all I wanted. But even if Gato and I had met alone, I doubt that I could have given outward expression to the joy I felt.

As soon as Master was back in the saddle, we moved along in a regular avalanche of horses and riders, whilst men and ladies stood up in cars, waving flags and handkerchiefs.

In the wild mix-up I lost sight of Gato, but after a while he again appeared beside me. To my surprise I saw that he was being ridden by a man who acted as if he were his owner. Obviously, my old pal was quite well again, for he jogged along as he had always done before. With every stride his ears flopped forward and backwards like loose straps on a saddle-bag, and his wavy black mane fluttered as his head and neck moved up and down.

Being unable to talk to me just then, he looked at me through the corner of his near eye, and when I caught his glances I couldn't believe that we had been separated for so long; the Past and the Present seemed like a succession of crazy dreams.

I don't remember for how long we were in the midst of the noisy crowd, but I vividly recall entering a big city where people cheered us from the pavement and windows.

At last we halted in a courtyard where a number of horses'

heads peeped at us from their stalls. Only a few members of the crowd were with us now, but outside, in the street, I could still hear the noise of the multitude which had accompanied us. As soon as the saddle had been taken off me, I was given a drink of water, and then I was led into a loose-box. Presently Gato was brought in by a groom; and we both gave sighs of relief when the door was closed, and the two of us were alone. Whilst we sniffed one another, Master and several men watched us, but very soon they disappeared, whereupon Gato and I were able to talk things over in peace.

Story Twenty-Two

*Happy Gato, re-united with his old friends, talks about
Mexico City and things he saw and heard there. The
journey is resumed, and the ten-footed expedition arrives
in Texas*

MANCHA has already told you how we met again after our
separation, so I'll not bore you with a long story about how I
felt when I suddenly saw my two old friends among that crowd
outside the city.

The man who rode on me at the time wasn't my new master,
as Mancha had suspected, but just a friend who had been very
good and kind to me whilst I was ill. When I was well enough
to go out into the parks, it was he who came with me, and when
all the *charros* rode out of the city to meet Master and Mancha,
my new friend took me with him.

You can easily imagine what a grand time the two of us had
in that stable. For hours on end we chatted about this and that,
my pal being often fast asleep when I still talked to him. Poor
fellow; he had travelled hundreds of miles since I had left him,
and I didn't begrudge him his well-earned rest!

I guessed that we wouldn't stay in the stable very long, for
Master and Mancha had only rested two or three days when we
were taken out for long trots; obviously to keep us in training.

I wish you could have seen some of the public receptions we
were given in Mexico City. Every day Mancha and I were taken

to places where merry crowds gathered, and bands played to make things more jolly.

Daring Mexican cowboys displayed their skill with ropes and horses, and dashing policemen showed us what can be done on motor-cycles; and there were speeches and dancing, and even bull-fights, which Mexicans love.

I didn't know what a bull-fight was till we were taken to a huge arena where we were shown to the biggest crowd of people I had ever seen.

I could tell that Master didn't like going to the bull-fight, but as he was the guest of Mexico he had to do as the Mexicans do.

It seems that it is a great honour to perform the opening ceremony of a bull-fight; and as Master was asked to do this, he couldn't very well refuse without offending his many friends; so, mounted on Mancha, he rode out into a big sandy circle, which was surrounded by many people who—from a distance—looked like ants; but made the noise of a thunder-storm.

There was something about the place that made me feel very uneasy and nervous, and I noticed that Mancha was affected in the same way, for when he was out in the middle of the arena he pranced about so much that I thought he was going to buck.

A little later a band began to play, and Master led in a procession of men who were dressed in beautiful costumes, the gold and silver adornments on them glittering in the brilliant sunshine.

As soon as my two friends were out of the arena, and back with me, a bugle-call was heard, whereupon a trap-door opened, and a beautiful black bull raced into the ring. Surprised at the strange scene around him, he suddenly stopped to see what all

Dancing the *Jarabe del Tapatío;* the national dance of Mexico

this might mean; but just then one of the men in a gold and silver costume, ran in front of him, waving a red cloak, which so infuriated the bull that he scratched the ground and threw sand on his back.

I will say nothing about what I saw later, for it was so disgusting and horrible that Master led us to a yard behind the arena where he tied us to a rail.

Quite a number of other horses were tied in a row alongside us, and when I looked at them more carefully I saw that most of them were very old, some being veritable skeletons.

Next to me stood a chestnut who must have been a fine horse when he was young, but now he was so thin that one could count all his ribs, sticking out under a hide which was dry and parched like old leather. The poor old horse's legs were sagging at the knees, and he looked so sad that I spoke to him to cheer him up a little.

At first he took no notice, but after a while he answered, and later told me a story which was so pitiful that it haunts me to this day.

My poor friend told me that he was born on a beautiful estate in a country called America. He had had a happy youth, for the fields in which he played were green, and the people who owned him said he was the sweetest little pet.

When he was grown-up he was sold to the army; and had to learn many things. For several years he served his country faithfully and well, and then, one day, he and many of his companions were sold to the Mexican army. My new friend told me how he had fought in several revolutions; and he showed me the scars of some old wounds.

Having become too old for fighting, he was sold to a peasant, who only paid a few silver coins for him. Out in a semi-desert he starved and worked hard for several months; but, with the bad treatment and advancing age, he became so shaky and feeble that it had been very painful and difficult for him to walk into the city; he was sold to the owner of the bull-ring.

The unfortunate horse was weak and spoke very slowly, for he had been in this yard for two days without food or drink.

At last I began to understand why my poor friend and the other horses were there; and I felt like kicking the whole arena to smithereens when I thought that all these poor old animals had fought, worked and suffered for men. All they had expected for their faithful services was to be treated kindly in their old age; but although they were fully entitled to this, the reward they were to get was to be gored to death by a bull who would never harm them without being driven to it by man; and yet he likes to call us horses his "friends."

My neighbour hadn't quite finished his story when men rushed up to saddle him, and as soon as this had been done, a man who was dressed in a colourful costume, mounted. A lance was then handed to the rider who immediately dug his cruel spurs into the hollow flanks of my friend; he was so shaky on his legs that he tottered and swayed. A man then dragged him along by the bridle, whilst another followed behind, beating the wretched animal with a stick.

I watched my poor friend stagger down a dark passage under the grandstand, and when a gate was swung open I caught a glimpse of the sun-lit arena where two dead horses lay, their glassy eyes staring towards heaven, as if asking for justice. On the far side of the sandy ring I could see the bull, whose tongue hung out of his foaming mouth as he stood panting for breath, whilst blood streamed down his sturdy neck.

For a second or two I got a glimpse of a mass of humanity whose yells and cheers sounded like the breaking of mighty waves against cliffs on the seashore. As the gate closed I saw

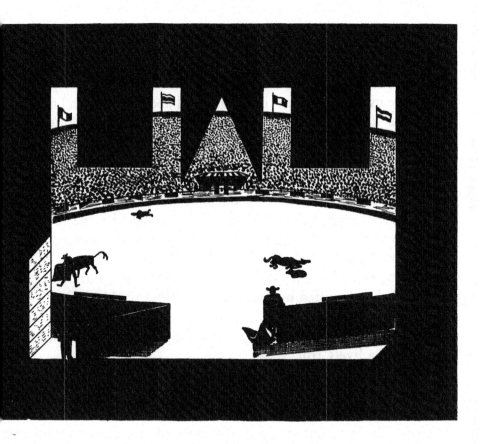

the bull raise his head and look at my trembling friend who stood there, swaying to and fro, meekly waiting for the only reward he could expect from despotic and cruel Man.

The big gate creaked as it was closed; and soon after I heard a vicious snort which was followed by a dull thud, thereupon Master rushed us back to the stable, where people were kind to us.

．　　　．　　　．　　　．　　　．　　　．

The rest had done Mancha so much good that he became very frisky, and sometimes even naughty, for whenever Master came to give us our daily exercise he pranced about, and even bucked.

One day a big crowd of horsemen—who were dressed in Mexican costumes—came to the stable. When the saddles and packs had been strapped on us, we set out, accompanied by the riders who came with us until we were well out of the city.

I knew that we wouldn't return to the stable, for when Master had said "good-bye" to all his friends who had come to show us the way out of Mexico City, they galloped away and were soon out of sight behind a cloud of dust.

Master stood staring in the direction of the city, and he looked so sad that I sniffed his face to cheer him up. He pulled himself together with a jerk, and having re-adjusted the pack and tightened our girths, swung into the saddle and guided us north at a lively trot.

I was glad to be out in the open, and once more with my two friends I had missed so terribly during my illness. Now, as we trotted along, I felt my old self again. As soon as we had settled down to our swinging trot, and I heard the dull thud of our hoofs on the sandy road, I even forgot the stable.

Master, too, seemed to have cheered up, for very soon the regular jolts of trotting, and the drumming of eight hoofs, made him hum tunes I hadn't heard since I fell ill at the border of Guatemala.

As usual, when he was happy and well, Mancha grunted and snorted as he jogged along, and every time he took a deep breath I heard the creaking of the saddle—a noise I now even liked.

The rays of the sinking sun had tinted the sandy plain with gold, when we sighted the low square houses of a village where we hoped Master intended to spend the night. We hurried our steps, and when the sun dipped behind the mountains in the west, we clattered over the rough cobble-stones of the main street where people had assembled to see us arrive.

Until late that night, men in loose-fitting white clothes and huge hats came to look at us, and a band of eight or nine musicians made ear-splitting noises. The fellow with the piccolo tried to make himself heard above the man with a battered bass trumpet, who seemed to be competing against a strong-armed peasant, thumping a big drum with all his might.

Although the music wasn't pleasant to the ear, everybody seemed to enjoy it, and even Master—who constantly yawned—was with the merry throng until he could only keep his eyes open with difficulty.

When the sun rose over the mountains in the east we were on our way again, following a wide sandy trail which led straight north down a vast valley which looked like a big semi-desert.

Cactuses, small scraggy palm-trees and shrubs were the only

plants which seemed to thrive there; and water was conspicuous by its absence.

At long intervals we came to humble settlements or villages where people were very hospitable.

We were usually put into the back yard of the local police-station; but if there wasn't one, Master slept on the ground near us, to make sure that horse thieves would keep away.

Years before we passed through these now abandoned regions, farms and even big stables had existed here and there; but during the many terrible revolutions, they had been destroyed, and even the water-wells had been made useless.

Sometimes the weather was very cold, strong winds, and once even snow and sleet, adding to our discomforts. This happened on Christmas eve. We had been on the move since early morning, and hadn't seen a living being all day. Many miles of semi-desert were behind us when we saw what looked like a house in the distance. The wind whistled through our manes and tails, driving along snow and sleet which, as it hit us, felt as if we were being whipped.

The thought that we would soon find shelter, food and water, cheered us up; but on arriving at the house we were disappointed to find it abandoned and in ruins.

It would have been foolish to continue our journey, for it was already beginning to get dark, so Master unsaddled us in a corner of what had once been a large room. There, at least, we were sheltered from the cutting wind, which continued to blow in all its fury.

Upon investigating the ruined well, Master discovered that there was a little water at the bottom, so he placed a stone in his sombrero and lowered it into the well by means of his lasso. Although the water was bad, we were glad to drink it, and when Master discovered an old mattress which was stuffed with straw, we were simply delighted, for in spite of the fact that half of it was burnt, and had a nasty taste, we had something with which to fill our empty bellies.

After a careful search through the saddle-bags and pack, Master found some old bread-crusts, which he started to gnaw as a hungry hare might the tough roots of a tree.

Many miles away from the nearest living being we spent our Christmas eve, the flickering light of a tiny fire making the ruined place look uncanny. The wind sang mournful carols through the holes which had once been windows, but in spite of the moans, hoots and howls, Master curled up in his blankets and slept, while we dozed near him.

For hundreds of miles we went north through the vast valley. At long intervals we came to two or three towns, but in villages, and out in the open, we had to put up with many discomforts. The revolution was still in full swing, and bandits made certain regions very unsafe.

. . . .

A Chinese merchant is said to have been travelling over a plain with laden mules when he was held up by a number of soldiers. The two armies who were fighting at the time called themselves *Federales* and *Revolucionarios*. But as they had no distinctive uniforms, or none at all, it was impossible to tell to which body the soldiers belonged.

"Quien vive?" ("Who goes there?") a gruff voice demanded of

the startled Chinaman, who answered in a faltering voice, "Fede*l*ales," pronouncing the "r" as "l," as most Chinamen do, because the rolling "r" doesn't exist in their native tongue.

The trembling merchant had hardly finished his answer when the soldiers pounced on him, and having taken everything he possessed, they chased him away over the plain. As it happened, these soldiers belonged to the party of the *Revolucionarios;* and our poor friend—the Chinaman—had guessed wrong in saying "Fede*l*ales."

Thankful to be still alive, the unfortunate Chinaman tottered over the plain, when he was again stopped by a band of soldiers who had been hiding behind some big cactus plants.

"Quien vive?" they demanded in chorus, whereupon the Chinaman immediately answered "*L*evoluciona*l*ios." But again he had guessed the wrong pass-word; for, as bad luck would have it, these soldiers were *Federales*. Before the unlucky Chinaman had time to correct his mistake, he was beaten and chased away like a stray dog.

Nursing his bruised body, and cursing his ill-fortune, he continued his weary tramp over the plain, when he was again held up by a band of soldiers who demanded the pass-word.

Unable to decide whether to say *Revolucionarios* or *Federales*, but to make quite certain to be on the safe side, the Chinaman said, "You tellee me first and I tellee you after."

.   .   .   .

We were luckier than the Chinaman of this story; for, instead of robbing and beating us, all the soldiers were very friendly.

Once a great number of cavalry-men and officers accompanied

us for a long distance, and when we reached the top of a "*loma*" (low hill), the commander pointed ahead, where we saw cavalry in the distance. The commander of our escort told Master that he could accompany us no further, for the soldiers we saw were enemies, and if the two bodies met there would be fireworks.

Having taken our leave—during the performance of which bottles were taken out of saddle-bags and handed round—we trotted away, and were soon received by the "enemies," the commander warmly embracing Master, whose sun-burnt face hadn't seen a razor for a week.

As if by magic, bottles appeared everywhere, and when every man had swallowed a few gulps of *mescal,* as strong Mexican brandy is called, we rode towards the headquarters of our new escort. Wrapped in a thick cloud of dust, we cantered over the sandy track, and when we arrived at our destination we were given a welcome bath and as much fodder as we could eat.

We continued to travel north for many days, and finally came to the end of the Valley of Mexico, which is high above sea-level. We were still up on the *mesa,* as the Mexican table-land is called, but now we headed in the direction of some rugged mountains, the ridges of which had all sorts of strange shapes.

We weren't always accompanied, for most of the time we travelled alone, Master guessing the way as best he could.

One day we saw a solitary cow in the distance; and as she appeared to be very agitated about something, the three of us watched her with curiosity. I noticed that she repeatedly charged some big black buzzards which had congregated near a cluster of bushes, in and out of which the cow dashed furiously, bellowing as she chased the birds who hovered close over her head.

I was just thinking that Master wasn't wise in approaching closer, when the scraggy, long-horned cow saw us. For a moment she raised her head and lashed the air with her tail, and then, without further warning, charged us with the speed of a stag. Before Master had time to draw his revolver, the infuriated animal was on us, and although I tried to dodge her, one of the horns grazed my left flank, nearly knocking Master out of the saddle. Wise old Mancha wasn't slow in realising the danger, and quickly galloped out of harm's way.

The cow was just turning to charge me again, when Master's revolver spat fire, barking twice in quick succession. Almost at the same instant the cow's legs seemed to give way under her, and she rolled over on the ground within two or three yards of me.

To make quite sure that the animal should give no more trouble, Master fired two more shots into her head from close range, whereupon he quickly dismounted to examine my wound, which, fortunately, wasn't a serious one.

When he was called, Mancha came trotting back to us; and while the first-aid equipment was taken out of the saddle-bags he kept a weather-eye on the dead cow, every now and again snorting, as if trying to tell her that she was no lady.

When Master had disinfected my superficial wound, and the blood had stopped oozing out of it, we went to the bushes to find out what had so infuriated the cow.

When Master had fired his revolver, a number of buzzards had risen into the air, and were now circling above us.

We hadn't to search long to solve the mystery, for on the ground lay a dead calf whose body had already been badly mutilated by the birds, and who were now waiting for us to go away to finish their repast.

I was glad when we left this scene of tragedy behind us; and, as I watched the buzzards swoop down towards the cluster of bushes, I thought that I was lucky not to be there as an extra big feed for them.

. By following a trail which led through a winding valley between high rocky mountains, we finally entered a vast plain which can almost be called a desert. All we saw there was sand, parched dry by the hot rays of the sun, and here and there patches of scraggy shrubs, and then more sand. Wind devils danced about like gigantic black ghosts; and occasionally we passed the bleached bones of an animal, and then we again plodded over seemingly endless stretches of sand. This was the kind of country we went through until we saw a winding streak of silver, far ahead of us. A river; perhaps a cool drink—relief!

As we drew near, a dark cluster on the banks became clearer, until we saw that we were heading for a "pueblo" (town). But what was that cloud of dust ahead of us? Slowly it came towards us until, at last, we recognised the shapes of many horses and riders.

Although the sight of approaching horsemen wasn't a new one to us, we hesitated and sniffed the air with dilated nostrils, but, in answer to our nervous snorts, Master urged us on. The uncomfortable atmosphere of revolution had gradually worked on our nerves. Both Mancha and I felt that Master had been very excited for the last day or two, and we noticed that he gazed at the horizon with more keenness than he had ever shown before.

With loud cheers the horsemen came dashing towards us, and when they were so close that we could smell the odour of sweaty leather, they suddenly brought their mounts to a standstill, in doing so throwing up so much dust that horses and men were hardly visible.

While we pranced about and reared up, the leader of this band of horsemen came forward, whereupon Master leapt out of the saddle to embrace the man, as is customary among friends in Mexico.

While all the dashing riders cheered and waved their big hats in the air, Master and his new friend mounted. Soon after we continued our march towards the river, the merry and boisterous cavalcade following behind us, hundreds of hoofs rumbling on the sandy soil.

When we entered the little town we were greeted by music; and, as we marched along, headed by a brass band, we were cheered to the echo by crowds who lined the streets.

Our procession finally halted in front of a building in the *plaza* (square), whereupon a man made a speech from the balcony of a house. Mancha and I were so used to hearing speeches that we hardly listened, but we liked them all the same, for experience had taught us that whenever this happened we were in for an extra good feed.

At the time we didn't know that we had reached a place called Laredo, and that the land on the other side of the river is called Texas, which is part of the United States of America.

Two or three days later Master again put the saddles on us,

and having taken leave of his many friends, led us towards the river, across which there was a fine stone bridge.

We had hardly reached the other side when we were again greeted by a big crowd of people who didn't look a bit like the Mexicans and South Americans we were accustomed to. Somehow I felt as if I had entered into a new world, for everything I saw was different from anything I had ever seen before.

The houses were square and very high, and the streets were paved so smoothly that I had to take care not to slip. The people were white, and wore clothes like the ones I had seen in Buenos Aires. I seemed to recognise the sound of the language they spoke; for surely I had heard similar talk in Panama.

We were taken to a place where many soldiers lived, and there we were put into a lovely clean stable reminding us of days gone by.

Even if I tried, I couldn't tell you what a fine time we had in that place. Master seemed to be happier than he had ever been before; and every time he showed us to the crowds who came to visit us, he patted our necks with such pride that we wondered what we had done.

Soldiers who knew even more about our hoofs than Master did, greased, trimmed and shaped them for us; and we were washed, combed and brushed till the blood under our skins tingled, and Mancha's spotted coat glistened like a jaguar's.

We felt very proud when hundreds of soldiers paraded past us on a big field; but I'm sorry to say that Mancha's behaviour on that occasion wasn't what it ought to have been, for he was so full of oats that he insisted on showing it by prancing along

o

sideways and snorting in his worst Patagonian slang.

A few days later a cavalry detachment accompanied us out of the army post, and when the officer in command raised an arm, the men halted. As soon as Master had taken leave of the commander, the soldiers swung round their mounts, and returned in the direction we had come from.

Once more the three of us were left alone; and I wondered where we would go next.

STORY TWENTY-THREE

Mancha's journey to the end of the trail. He separates and re-unites with Gato. The travellers' return to the pampas. Trapalanda

I'M not going to tell you much about our journey through the United States. If I did, I'm afraid you'd be bored. For even though we had to travel well over two thousand miles, one day was much like another.

We just trotted along the grassy sides of concrete roads; miles and miles of monotony, with countless cars speeding past. Wherever we stopped we met crowds of people who had come to have a look at us, and we were given so many and such good things to eat that the girths began to feel tight around our bellies.

In some parts the country was beautiful, but there were so many advertising posters on both sides of the road that we could hardly see the scenery beyond them.

We passed through countless villages, towns and cities; and, if it hadn't been for thousands of speeding cars, we might have enjoyed ourselves.

Sometimes the trotting on hard and slippery roads was unpleasant, and made our feet very tired.

We got so used to the heavy and speedy traffic, that we didn't even blink when a car shot past us like a flash of lightning; but, after Gato and I had been hit and nearly crippled, we took good

care to jump out of the way when a car was driven too close to us.

Oh, how I hated some of these nasty motorists! And how I wished that Master would scare them away by shooting into the air, as he had sometimes done to frighten monkeys in the jungle!

After weeks of travelling we came to a big town near which we stayed on a beautiful farm.

When Master came to saddle up, I was surprised to see that he didn't bring the old pack; and, when I was ready to start, I could hardly believe my eyes when I observed a man who led Gato towards a lovely green field near the house. I heard Master say good-bye to my pal, and then he mounted and made me trot away.

I felt very strange without Gato; but when I thought over things, I realised that Master no longer needed a pack, for where-ever we stopped he could buy what he needed.

Travelling with two horses among all the traffic had been awkward and even dangerous.

I didn't know that we had nearly reached our goal; that saddles and packs would soon become memories, and that, be-fore long, I would be on the way back to my beloved pampas—home!

.   .   .   .

Now I will tell you something about the strangest place I saw on our long journey.

We had been on the march so long, and I had seen and heard so much that I began to think I couldn't learn much more, and that there were but few things I hadn't seen in this world.

However, one day I found out that I had been quite wrong in thinking so, for we came to a most extraordinary and terrifying place which I will now try to describe.

We had penetrated into some canyons which became deeper and deeper as we advanced. On both sides of us, perpendicular walls towered high into the sky; and when I looked up and saw clouds drifting by, the giddy walls of rock seemed to be swaying, as if about to fall and bury us.

Deafening noise of thunder, and the sight of these awe-inspiring precipices, made my brain whirl till I thought I was dreaming a strange dream. To feel Master's weight on my back was very comforting, and I mechanically went in the direction he guided me. He must have realised that I was afraid and bewildered, for every now and again he leaned forward in the saddle and patted my neck.

I was almost giddy with fear, so I just pranced along, trembling and sweating, and snorting at the strange things I saw.

Sometimes I thought I was in a wild and thundering mountain river which tossed about tree-trunks and rocks, hurtling them downstream along the bottom of the deep canyon.

Above the unearthly din I heard many strange and blood-curdling noises which sounded like the roaring of lions, snarls of jaguars, bellowing of bulls, honking of wild geese, loud agonised bleatings of sheep, yells like the war-cries of Indians and snorts of wild stallions. To render this frightful noise more jarring to my ears, it was accompanied by continuous rumblings, like those of a landslide, and throaty snarls which reminded me of pumas facing each other before fighting out a dispute over a kill.

On what appeared to be the banks of the torrent, masses of natives moved about, the women's gaily-coloured clothes and painted faces contrasting strangely with the unearthly scenes and din around them. Presently I began to realise that I was in no immediate danger of being killed, and therefore observed things a little more closely.

To my amazement I noticed that the rocky walls of the canyon were hollow, and that they were full of countless square holes, not unlike windows. I began to wonder if these canyons were inhabited by cave-dwellers, when I came to a place where I saw what looked like the entrance to an underground cave. I could hardly believe my eyes when I saw hundreds of people rush into it, whilst a stream of hustling natives came out.

Upon closer examination I noticed that men and women went through entrances which appeared to lead into the interior of the rocky walls; and looking up, I saw what seemed to be human heads, peeping out of the many square holes in the side of the perpendicular chasm.

I was just trying to solve the mystery of the underground cave when a terrific noise drowned all the others, and made me prop and snort.

In front of me, from one side of the canyon to the other, there was a structure which looked like a bridge. Suddenly, something like a huge black snake—with many shiny eyes all along the body—whizzed over it, making such a noise that I almost froze with fear.

Only when Master gently dug his heels into my ribs, I realised that I was awake and not dreaming, and continued to pick my way along the bottom of the canyon.

After some time I got so used to the noise and strange scenes around me that I lost all fear, and therefore was able to think clearly.

By degrees I realised that I was moving along the streets of a huge city, and that the rocky walls of the canyons were part of colossal houses which men call *skyscrapers*. All the terrific noises were caused by thousands of cars, trucks and other vehicles which moved along like a mass of drift-wood in a mountain river after a storm. The terrifying snake-like monster was an elevated train which had crossed the bridge with the speed of an arrow.

When I came to an open space, I had a good view of the imposing buildings which towered high into the sky. The golden rays of the evening sun glittered on the pointed steel domes with which some of the skyscrapers were adorned, giving them the appearance of gigantic spear-heads which seemed to be piercing the red clouds which slowly drifted past them.

Whilst looking at the breath-taking sights these masses of steel and concrete presented, I didn't realise that we had reached our final goal; that this was New York—the end of our long, long trail!

.   .   .   .

Guided by mounted policemen, Master and I arrived at the port where I was ferried out to an island on which many soldiers lived.

Looking out of my stable, I could see the amazing city quite close across the water. When night fell, thousands of lights

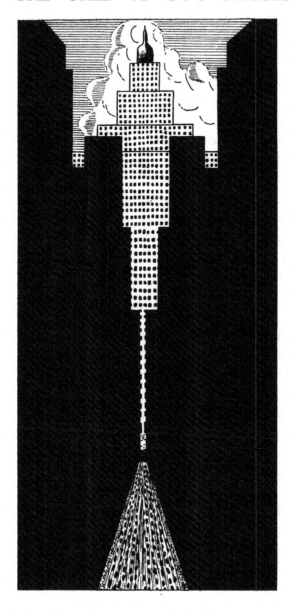

illuminated the skyscrapers which seemed to touch the moon. The mass of lights, together with the twinkling stars of a perfect autumn night, reflected on the water which separated me from the land; and to give life to this picture of a strange Fairyland, ocean liners and many boats glided over the vibrating sheet of silver.

When I listened to the distant rumble of traffic, I was reminded of the grim struggle that goes on behind this man-made curtain of light.

The inky blackness of a jungle night may have its terrors, and may hide the tragedies of Nature fighting for life; but behind the merry lights of a city you will find more cruelty, suffering and injustice than in the darkness of the most forbidding jungle, where Nature, and not Man, rules supreme.

.   .   .   .

I had a most enjoyable time in my new stable, and a grand surprise when old Gato appeared.

When I listened to his account of how he had come by train, and he told me about the soft time he had had whilst Master and I plodded on towards our goal, I almost envied him.

The two of us were taken to all sorts of places where thousands of people stared at us; and one day, a man who must have been very important, pinned a lovely gold medal on Master's breast.

Later on this happened several times; and we often wondered what he had done to deserve so much gold and gaily-coloured ribbons. But as they seemed to please him greatly, we didn't begrudge them to him; for, in any case, we couldn't have eaten them, and therefore they would have been of no use to us.

One day, we were put into big wooden boxes and gently hoisted on to a big ship. Soon the skyscrapers seemed to be moving away from us, and an hour or two later we were out on the ocean; heading south. One day followed another, and still we were kept in our boxes. Every time Master came to see us, we thought we would be let out, but all he did was to bring us a lump of sugar or some other tit-bit.

There were lots of people on this ship, and all day long a regular procession of smartly-dressed ladies and men came to look at us. We were given so many lumps of sugar that we got sick of eating them, and as our only fodder was hay, bran and oats, we were longing for a good feed of juicy grass.

We must have been on board two solid weeks when we sighted land. Even though the ship stopped at a port for a day, we weren't taken off, but had to stay where we were.

For twenty days we travelled south; and then something seemed to tell us that we were nearing home. When we sighted the green shores of the Argentine we felt like jumping off the ship, and swimming ashore; but, as this was impossible, we had to wait for another day till the ship had slowly steamed up the wide and yellow River Plate.

Hundreds of people were assembled on the docks, and before we knew what was happening, a wild crowd came up the gang-way, and rushed towards us to pat our heads and necks. With all the excitement and shouting, we didn't notice for a while that some people were cutting hair off our tails which stuck out of the boxes, as we backed away from all the outstretched hands.

I hardly remember how I was taken off the ship, for when I

could again think clearly, I found myself in a stable which seemed very familiar. After the crowd had gone, leaving Gato and me alone, we had a good look round the place.

What a surprise we had! As if by magic, we had returned to the first stable we had ever been in; well over two years ago, when we had come to Buenos Aires from the wilds of Patagonia!

I'll not attempt to tell you how happy we were, for even if I tried, my horse language would fail me.

Every day crowds of people came to look at us; men made speeches, and bands played. But as we couldn't understand half of what the orators said, we were rather bored with these functions.

At the end of a few days we were taken to a railway station where we were loaded on a train which soon rumbled out of the city.

We had travelled about five hours when we began to recognise the country; and as we looked out between the bars of the railway wagon we saw a vast grassy plain over which roamed horses and cattle.

When, at last, the train stopped at the little prairie station and we were let out, we looked round and sniffed the air. The cowboys who watched us were surprised to see us gallop straight towards the gate of our well-remembered field, and when we stopped and called our friends who were grazing in the distance, the men's surprise changed into amazement.

Although we had been away for many months, and in spite of having travelled through strange lands, we had not forgotten the place where we made friends with Master.

The old corral was still there; but now we wouldn't have

minded much if we had again been put into it, for the place looked and smelt like home.

As soon as one of the cowboys had opened the gate, we dashed into the field, and raced up to our friends who looked at us with surprise. Some had forgotten us, but very soon we renewed our old friendship with them.

We wondered what had become of Master, for we hadn't seen him since we were put on the train in Buenos Aires. For two long days we kept looking for him, but on the third morning after our return, he suddenly appeared riding on a horse we didn't know. It took us some time before we believed our eyes and noses, for we had never seen Master ride on another horse.

After that he came to visit us every day; and we enjoyed it when he patted our necks and scratched our noses. We used to sniff him all over, and nuzzled his pockets in which he usually had a few lumps of sugar, or some other tit-bit we were fond of.

One day he visited us several times, and we were surprised when he came again, late in the evening.

With the red light of the setting sun, the pampas looked like a rolling sea of gold. The only sounds to break the peaceful silence were the rustling of the grass and the munching of our grazing herd.

As Master approached, a *tero-tero* rose into the air, its shrill cry of alarm contrasting strangely with the peaceful surroundings.

When our old friend had dismounted, we both went to sniff him; and as he seemed to be sad, we rubbed our noses against him. He sat down on the ground, and whilst we ate the lumps of sugar he gave us, we softly nickered into his ears, asking for more.

For a long time he sat with us; and when the sun was beginning to dip into the vast ocean of the pampas, he quietly rose, and, having patted our necks, went up to his horse and leapt into the saddle.

He hadn't galloped far when he reined in his mount, and turning in the saddle called: "*Good-bye, Mancha and Gato!*" He looked just as we had always known him; but somehow I couldn't help feeling that something was on his mind.

With a wave of his battered old sombrero, out of which we had had many a good feed, he swung his horse round again, and galloped towards the setting sun. As he went away he looked smaller and smaller, until we could only see a speck at the horizon; and when the last after-glow of red had faded away, Master was but a memory.

.   .   .   .

The gauchos say that far beyond the place where the sun sets there begins a long, long trail which leads away to the West. Once a horse is on that trail there's no turning back, and he must follow it until he comes to a high mountain which opens as he approaches, and silently closes again when he has passed through the entrance which looks like a huge gate.

Immediately the horse breathes the cool air of *Trapalanda*— as the gauchos call this heaven for horses—he becomes young again; and all the hardships, sufferings and injustices he has endured in this world are forgotten. Full of vigour and joy, he gallops into this endless prairie where the grasses are always green and sweet, and where only men who have loved horses in this world are allowed to enter.

I hope the gauchos are right, for I'd like to meet the thousands and thousands of good horses who have served their masters faithfully and well. I'd like to meet all who in their innocence were ill-treated, and those who have helped emperors, kings and soldiers to fulfil their worldly ambitions. Men have built monuments to many of their heroes, but in their vanity they have forgotten all about the horses who have suffered hardships for them without more hope of reward than to be treated kindly and well.

Some day, when we shall have seen our last sunset, we hope to be re-united with all our old friends, and that you will come to visit us—in *Trapalanda*.

Until then, farewell!

UNITED STATES OF AMERICA

New York

Washington

ATLANTIC OCEAN

Rio Grande

Laredo

CUBA

HAITI

MEXICO

Mexico

JAMAICA

GUATEMALA
SAN SALVADOR
HONDURAS
NICARAGUA
COSTA RICA
PANAMA

Guatemala

Colon

VENEZUELA

R. Orinoco

GUIANAS

COLOMBIA

Equator

Quito

ECUADOR

Amazon River

PERU

BRAZIL

PACIFIC OCEAN

Lima

Cuzco

BOLIVIA

PARAGUAY

Rio

CHILE

R. Paraguay

URUGUAY

Buenos Aires

ARGENTINE

Here Mancha and Gal
are spending their old age.

Approximate size of
England, Wales and Scotland
on the same scale

Other titles in the Equestrian Travel Classic series published by
The Long Riders' Guild Press. We are constantly adding to our
collection, so for an up-to-date list please visit our website:
www.thelongridersguild.com

The Long Riders' Guild
The world's leading source of information regarding equestrian exploration!
www.thelongridersguild.com

CPSIA information can be obtained
at www.ICGtesting.com
Printed in the USA
LVOW13*0721301017

554270LV00011B/116/P